Rave Reviews

Julie Schwendimann

VP GSS Operations
Stanley Black & Decker

"Jenn skillfully delves into the critical behaviors that leaders must adopt to inspire and motivate their teams. From effective communication to fostering a culture of trust and collaboration, she leaves no stone unturned, offering 'practical' advice that can be 'readily' applied in various leadership scenarios."

Matt Barkley

Chief Human Resources Officer
Great Southern Wood Preserving, Inc

"As a coach, Jenn is like a best friend who tells you like it is in the spirit of helping you become the best leader you can be. She has been that 'best friend' for myself and several of my leaders over the years and her positive impact on business is substantial. Jenn is bold and direct, relatable, and real, this new book is simple to understand, realistic in its intention, and ultimately impactful when applied."

Max K.

Executive Leadership, Advertising

"The *ABC Playbook for Leadership Success* underscores the importance of building meaningful connections. Jenn explores the power of networking, mentorship, and empathy, guiding readers on how to establish and nurture relationships that can propel both personal and professional growth. Her insights into fostering consistent and empowering environments make this book even more relevant for modern day leaders."

Judith Colemon Kinebrew

Coach, Educator, Author, Facilitator

"What sets this book apart is its interactive nature. Throughout the chapters, Jenn incorporates exercises and reflection prompts that encourage readers to apply the concepts directly to their own experiences. These hands-on activities help bridge the gap between theory and practice, enabling readers to see immediate results in their leadership journey."

Charity Barnes

Group Vice President, CIO/CISO
Toyota Tsusho America Inc.

"What sets The *ABC Playbook for Leadership Success* apart is Jenn's unique approach to leadership, focusing on three fundamental pillars: Awareness, Behaviors, and Connections. Jenn masterfully intertwines these essential elements, empowering readers to cultivate a holistic understanding of what it takes to lead with excellence, truly transforming work relationships for positive impacts, and successfully empowering the magical work/life balance for those that embrace the concepts."

Jessica Lindquist

Vice President, Consumer Marketing

"Jenn's The *ABC Playbook for Leadership Success: Awareness, Behaviors, and Connections* is an outstanding resource that redefines the way we approach leadership. This book helped me professionally, and as a mother, wife, and friend. From further developing my growth mindset to improving my communication skills, Jenn's words and coaching continue to drive my success. Jenn has helped me become a more accountable, empathetic and results driven leader."

Anita McGorty

Executive Vice President
Association of National Advertisers

"Jenn's leadership approaches are game changers. Her guidance has enabled me to be a better leader, teammate, and business partner. Her introspective exercises for identifying what motivates people, including yourself, unearths insights for how to best lead and partner for optimal outcomes and strong working relationships, while her collection of practical strategies for navigating complex business challenges, dynamics, and situations helps drive success, delivered with confidence."

Kim Fitzpatrick

Life Leadership and Executive Business Coach

"Enough waiting around for good things to happen to you, it is the time to create it. The *ABC Playbook For Leadership Success* is an incredible resource that is truly the play by play to demonstrate that great things are achievable with really diving into the core principles in this compelling + resource rich guide. This leadership playbook brims with deep insight, practical application, and wisdom to truly help take you to the next level in all aspects of life and career. Wonderful work Jenn, this will be such a powerful tool for so many."

ABC
Playbook
for Leadership
Success

AWARENESS, BEHAVIORS, CONNECTIONS

JENNIFER CHLOUPEK, M.Ed.

DocUmeant *Publishing*

244 5th Avenue
Suite G-200
NY, NY 10001
646-233-4366

www.DocUmeantPublishing.com

Published by
DocUmeant Publishing
244 5th Avenue, Suite G-200
NY, NY 10001
646–233-4366

Cover Design by Patti Knoles | Edited by Ginger Marks

Illustrations and layout by DocUmeant Designs
www.DocUmeantDesigns.com

Library of Congress Cataloging-in-Publication Data

Names: Chloupek, Jennifer, author.
Title: ABC playbook for leadership success : awareness, behaviors, connections / Jennifer Chloupek.
Description: New York, NY : DocUmeant Publishing, [2023] | Summary: "This journal is designed to help you develop and enhance your leadership skills. In this journal, you will find a variety of activities and assessments that will help you gain a deeper understanding of yourself as a leader, and help you identify areas for growth and improvement. It can be used by you to enhance your skills and achieve your goals. Whether working alone or with a coach, the playbook can help you to identify your strengths and weaknesses, set priorities, and develop a roadmap for success. The ABC Playbook for Leadership Success is a versatile and powerful tool that can help YOU unlock your full potential and achieve your goals"-- Provided by publisher.
Identifiers: LCCN 2023020165 | ISBN 9781957832005 (paperback)
Subjects: LCSH: Leadership. | Executive ability.
Classification: LCC HD57.7 .C5168 2023 | DDC 658.4/092--dc23/eng/20230428
LC record available at https://lccn.loc.gov/2023020165

Contents

INTRODUCTION   IX

PART 1: CORE AWARENESS   1

Activity 1: Leadership Style Assessment 2

Activity 2: Core Values Assessment 4

Activity 3: Strengths and Weaknesses Assessment 7

Activity 4: Emotional Intelligence Assessment 9

PART 2: CORE BEHAVIORS   13

Activity 5: Active Listening Exercise 14

Activity 6: Communication Style Assessment 16

Activity 7: Growth vs. Fixed Mindset 18

Activity 8: Setting Expectations—4-Step Process 20

Activity 9: Feedback Exercise 21

Activity 10: Conflict Resolution Exercise 23

Activity 11: Control, Influence, Concern 26

Activity 12: Limiting Beliefs 27

PART 3: CORE CONNECTIONS   31

Activity 13: Vision Exercise 32

Activity 14: Collaboration 33

Activity 15: Energy and Time 35

Activity 16: Best Self/Worst Self 38

Activity 17: Trust 40

Activity 18: Accountability 43

Activity 19: Power, Influence & Negotiation 47

Activity 20: Team Leadership — Assessment 50

ADDITIONAL RESOURCES   55

Grow Model 55

Framework for Problem Solving 56

Framework for Decision Making 56

Feedback Exercise for Self 58

Change 61

Resilience 64

Powerful Coaching Questions 65

Sample Coaching Questions 67

COACHING SESSION NOTES   69

WEEKLY REFLECTIONS   91

Introduction

Welcome to the *ABC Playbook for Leadership Success*! This playbook is designed to help you develop and enhance your leadership skills. In this playbook, you will find a variety of activities and assessments that will help you gain a deeper understanding of yourself as a leader, and help you identify areas for growth and improvement.

Leadership is a complex and challenging responsibility, requiring a unique set of skills and qualities that must be developed and nurtured over time. This leadership playbook is a valuable tool that can be used by you to enhance your skills and achieve your goals. Whether working alone or with a coach, the playbook can help you to identify your strengths and weaknesses, set priorities, and develop a roadmap for success.

When used by yourself, you can use the *ABC Playbook for Leadership Success* to gain clarity on your leadership style, identify areas of improvement, and develop actionable strategies to achieve your goals. This playbook provides a structured approach to leadership development, guiding you through a process of self-reflection and goal setting that helps you to become more effective and efficient in your role as a leader.

Alternatively, when used with a coach, the *ABC Playbook for Leadership Success* can provide you with an additional layer of support and guidance. Coaches can help you to identify blind spots, provide feedback and insights, and hold you accountable for your progress. Together, you and your coach can work through the playbook, leveraging their expertise and knowledge to create a personalized development plan that addresses your specific needs and the needs of your organization. This playbook is a versatile and powerful tool that can help YOU unlock your full potential and achieve your goals.

The *ABC Playbook for Leadership Success* is divided into three main sections, each focusing on a different aspect of leadership: Core Awareness, Core Behaviors, and Core Connections. Each section contains multiple activities and assessments, and recommend you complete them in the order presented. The playbook is designed to be completed over a period of several weeks or months, and we encourage you to take your time and reflect deeply on each activity.

Enjoy the journey and trust the process!

Ground Rules:

Expectations:

COACH Acronym to assess leadership behaviors:

Communication:
How well do you communicate with your team? Do you actively listen and respond to your team's needs and concerns?

Openness:
Do you encourage open communication and transparency within your team? Do you value and consider different perspectives and ideas?

Accountability:
Do you hold yourself and your team accountable for their actions and decisions? Do you take responsibility for both successes and failures?

Coaching:
Do you actively coach and develop your team members? Do you provide feedback and guidance to help your team members grow and improve?

Humility:
Do you demonstrate humility and recognize your own limitations and mistakes? Do you admit when you don't know something and seek input from others?

Rate yourself on a scale from 1–5 on how you do with each leadership behavior.

1. Very Rarely: The behavior occurs extremely infrequently or not at all.
2. Rarely: The behavior occurs occasionally, but not frequently enough to be considered a regular habit.
3. Sometimes: The behavior occurs with some frequency but is not consistently present in my actions.
4. Often: The behavior is a regular habit and occurs frequently in my actions.
5. Very Often: The behavior is a consistent and frequent habit, occurring in my actions almost all the time.

REFLECTION: BASED ON THE ABOVE WHAT DO I PLAN TO DO?

Pre-Work

Instructions

1. On the next page, draw a river that tells your story, your leadership journey.
2. Start by drawing a wavy line across the center of the paper. This will represent the river.
3. Label the river with your name and write the date or time period that the journey covers.
4. Above the river, draw a symbol or image that represents the beginning of the journey. This could be a mountain, a tree, or any other object that has personal significance to you.
5. To your right and below the river, draw a symbol or image that represents the end of the journey. This could be a sunset, a finish line, or any other object that symbolizes completion or achievement.
6. On the river, draw several smaller symbols or images that represent significant events or milestones along the journey. These could be rocks, rapids, or other obstacles that you encountered and overcame. Label each of these with a brief description of what they represent.
7. Add some color to the drawing, using colored pencils or watercolors to make the symbols and images stand out.

Once the drawing is complete, you can use it to tell your leadership story, starting at the beginning and tracing your journey along the river. You can talk about the obstacles you faced, the lessons you learned, and the growth you experienced as a result. You can also use the drawing to illustrate how far you have come and the progress you have made.

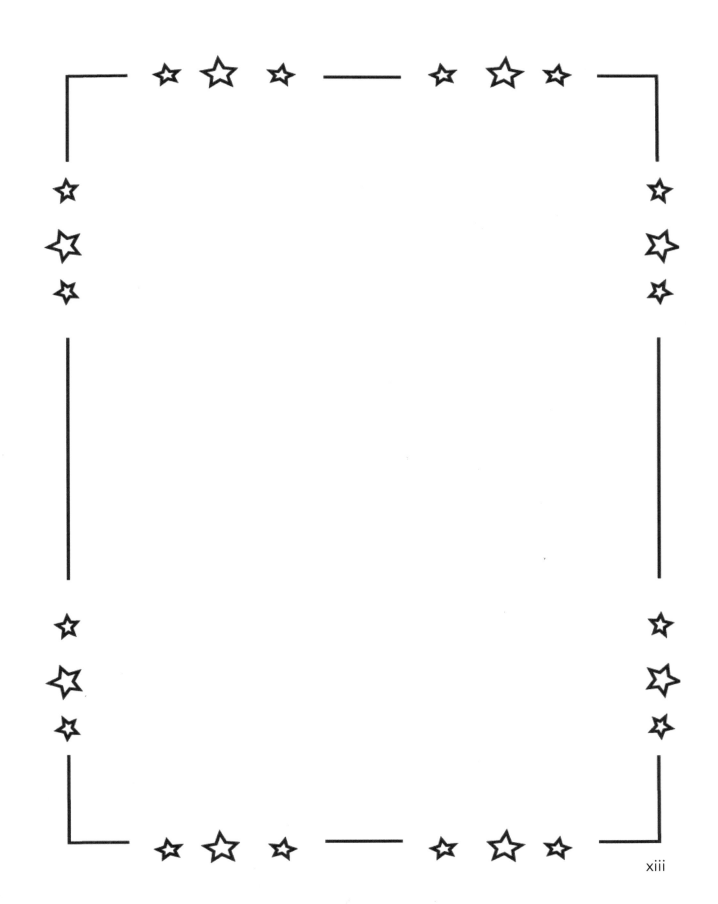

"THE UNEXAMINED
LIFE IS NOT
WORTH LIVING."

– SOCRATES

Part 1: Core Awareness

Activity 1: Leadership Style Assessment

Activity 2: Core Values Assessment

Activity 3: Strengths and Weaknesses Assessment

Activity 4: Emotional Intelligence Assessment

Activity 1: Leadership Style Assessment

This activity will help you identify your natural leadership style. You will complete a self-assessment, and then reflect on the results to gain a deeper understanding of your strengths and weaknesses as a leader.

Instructions: Read each statement carefully and select the answer that best represents your typical behavior or attitude. Choose the answer that you feel most closely aligns with your leadership style.

When faced with a challenge, I prefer to:
- a) Take charge and make quick decisions
- b) Collaborate with my team to come up with a solution
- c) Delegate the responsibility to someone else

In my team, I prefer to:
- a) Be the one who sets the vision and direction
- b) Encourage everyone to share their ideas and opinions
- c) Let everyone work independently with minimal supervision

When it comes to feedback, I:
- a) Give direct and constructive criticism
- b) Provide positive reinforcement and recognition for good work
- c) Avoid giving feedback altogether

When a team member is not meeting expectations, I:
- a) Hold them accountable and provide clear expectations
- b) Provide additional training or resources to help them improve
- c) Ignore the issue and hope it resolves itself

When making a decision, I:
- a) Rely on my own intuition and experience
- b) Weigh input and feedback from my team before making a decision
- c) Let someone else make the decision for me

When faced with a conflict within my team, I:
- a) Take charge and make a decision to resolve the conflict
- b) Facilitate a discussion to help the team come to a resolution
- c) Avoid the conflict altogether and hope it goes away

When it comes to setting goals, I:
- a) Set clear and ambitious goals for my team to work towards
- b) Collaborate with my team to set realistic and achievable goals
- c) Let my team set their own goals without much input from me

In my communication with my team, I:
- a) Speak clearly and confidently to ensure everyone understands my message
- b) Listen actively and encourage everyone to share their thoughts and ideas
- c) Keep communication to a minimum to avoid misunderstandings and conflicts

Scoring: For each question, assign yourself a point based on the following scale.

a) 3 points   b) 2 points   c) 1 point

Add up your total score and use the following guide to determine your leadership style.

20-24 points: Authoritative Leadership Style

15-19 points: Democratic Leadership Style

8-14 points: Laissez-Faire Leadership Style

Authoritative Leadership Style: You tend to be decisive, confident, and assertive in your leadership style. You take charge and set the vision and direction for your team and expect your team members to follow your lead. You provide clear guidance and expectations, and are not afraid to make tough decisions when necessary.

Democratic Leadership Style: You tend to be collaborative, supportive, and inclusive in your leadership style. You value input and feedback from your team and involve them in decision-making processes. You encourage open communication and prioritize the development and growth of your team members.

Laissez-Faire Leadership Style: You tend to be hands-off, laid back, and independent in your leadership style. You trust your team members to work independently and make their own decisions. You provide minimal guidance and supervision and allow your team members to take ownership of their work.

REFLECTION

Activity 2: Core Values Assessment

This activity will help you identify your core values as a leader. You will reflect on your own values, and then consider how these values influence your leadership style and decision-making.

ASSESSMENT FOR IDENTIFYING YOUR CORE VALUES

INSTRUCTIONS

On the following page you will find a list of *values*. Read each value carefully and rate how important it is to you on a scale of 1 to 5, with 1 being "not important at all" and 5 being "extremely important". Be honest with yourself and rate each value based on how you feel, not on how you think you should feel.

Value	Rating	Value	Rating
Achievement		Integrity	
Adventure		Justice	
Authenticity		Knowledge	
Balance		Leadership	
Creativity		Love	
Compassion		Loyalty	
Community		Open-mindedness	
Courage		Peace	
Curiosity		Personal development	
Education		Respect	
Family		Responsibility	
Freedom		Security	
Friendship		Self-discipline	
Growth		Service	
Happiness		Spirituality	
Health		Success	
Honesty		Teamwork	
Independence		Wealth	

Scoring: Once you have rated each value, add up your scores for each category to get a total score. Then, review the values with the highest scores to identify your core values.

SAMPLE SCORING TABLE

1-Not important at all 2-Slightly important 3-Moderately important 4-Very important 5-Extremely important

Value	Rating	Value	Rating
Achievement	4	Integrity	5
Adventure	3	Justice	4
Authenticity	5	Knowledge	5
Balance	2	Leadership	4
Creativity	4	Love	5
Compassion	5	Loyalty	4
Community	4	Open-mindedness	3
Courage	4	Peace	5
Curiosity	5	Personal development	4
Education	4	Respect	5
Family	5	Responsibility	5
Freedom	3	Security	3
Friendship	4	Self-discipline	4
Growth	4	Service	5
Happiness	5	Spirituality	3
Health	4	Success	4
Honesty	5	Teamwork	4
Independence	4	Wealth	2

Total Score: 153

Interpreting Your Results: The values with the highest scores represent your core values. In this example, the top five values are:

Authenticity | Compassion | Curiosity | Family | Honesty

These values are likely to be the most important to you and may be the driving force behind your decisions and actions. Understanding your core values can help you live a more fulfilling and meaningful life.

REFLECTION

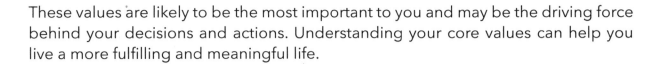

Activity 3: Strengths and Weaknesses Assessment

This activity will help you identify your strengths and weaknesses as a leader. You will complete a self-assessment, and then reflect on the results to gain a deeper understanding of your areas of expertise and areas for improvement.

STRENGTHS

Below is a list of possible strengths that you might exhibit. Circle your top 3 strengths or add strengths not listed and write them on the lines below.

Communication skills	Flexibility
Creativity	Initiative
Leadership	Resilience
Adaptability	Strategic thinking
Problem-solving	Decision-making
Positive attitude	Organizational skills
Time management	Analytical skills
Attention to detail	Perseverance
Empathy	Interpersonal skills
Teamwork	Resourcefulness

.... Top 3 Strengths.................

_____

_____

_____

WEAKNESSES

Below is a list of possible weaknesses that you might exhibit. Circle your top 3 weaknesses or add weaknesses not listed and write them on the lines below.

Lack of confidence

Procrastination

Poor time management

Difficulty prioritizing tasks

Disorganization

Poor communication skills

Inability to handle stress

Overthinking or analysis paralysis

Being too self-critical

Difficulty making decisions

Lack of assertiveness

Struggling with public speaking

Tendency to take on too much responsibility

Perfectionism

Impatience

Poor memory retention

Tendency to avoid confrontation

Difficulty with delegation

Tendency to jump to conclusions

Lack of empathy

.... Top 3 Weaknesses ....

_____

_____

_____

REFLECTION

Activity 4: Emotional Intelligence Assessment

Although the term Emotional Intelligence first appeared in 1964, it gained popularity by the 1995 best selling book *Emotional Intelligence* (EI) written by Daniel Goleman. Goleman defined EI as the skills and characteristics that drive leadership performance.

This activity will help you assess your emotional intelligence. You will reflect on your own emotional reactions and those of others and consider how this affects your leadership style and relationships with others. Using a Likert scale (1–5) or yes/no responses, rate yourself on each of these questions.

You can also ask colleagues or team members to rate you using the same questions to gather a 360-degree view of your emotional intelligence. The assessment results can help identify areas for improvement and provide insights for leadership development.

SELF-AWARENESS
- Do you have a good understanding of your emotions? ....
- Can you identify your strengths and weaknesses? ....
- Are you aware of how your emotions affect those around you?..........................

SELF-REGULATION
- Are you able to manage your emotions effectively? ....
- Do you remain calm in stressful situations? ....
- Can you control your impulses? ....

MOTIVATION

- Are you driven by a desire to achieve goals? ....
- Do you take initiative and act on opportunities? ....
- Are you able to bounce back from setbacks and failures? ....

EMPATHY

- Are you able to understand and relate to the emotions of others? ....
- Do you actively listen to others? ....
- Can you put yourself in someone else's shoes? ....

SOCIAL SKILLS

- Are you able to build and maintain positive relationships? ....
- Can you effectively communicate with others? ....
- Are you able to resolve conflicts and negotiate? ....

REFLECTION

Part 1: Core Aawareness Review

What have I learned and put into practice in Part 1: Core awareness?

....

....

....

....

What have I learned that I could do differently because of Part 1: Core awareness?

....

....

....

....

What will be my next steps? What can I start, stop, and continue to do?

....

....

....

....

"WHAT YOU DO
HAS FAR GREATER
IMPACT THAN
WHAT YOU SAY."

– STEPHEN COVEY, AUTHOR,
BUSINESSMAN AND SPEAKER

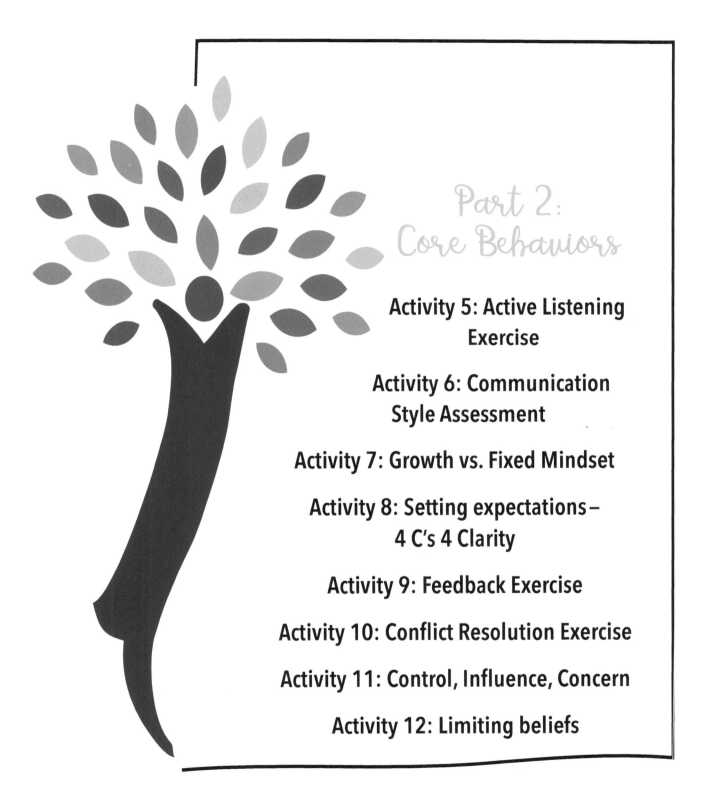

Part 2:
Core Behaviors

Activity 5: Active Listening Exercise

Activity 6: Communication Style Assessment

Activity 7: Growth vs. Fixed Mindset

Activity 8: Setting expectations – 4 C's 4 Clarity

Activity 9: Feedback Exercise

Activity 10: Conflict Resolution Exercise

Activity 11: Control, Influence, Concern

Activity 12: Limiting beliefs

Activity 5: Active Listening Exercise

This activity will help you develop your active listening skills. You will practice listening to others without interrupting and learn how to ask questions that encourage deeper understanding.

Active listening is a critical communication skill that involves fully engaging with and understanding what someone is saying. Here's an overview of how to actively listen.

1. Focus on the speaker: Give the speaker your full attention. Put aside any distractions, such as your phone or other devices, and maintain eye contact to show that you are fully present.
2. Avoid interrupting: Let the speaker finish their thoughts before responding. Interrupting can be disrespectful and can disrupt the flow of the conversation.
3. Show that you are listening: Use nonverbal cues, such as nodding or making eye contact, to show that you are engaged and actively listening.
4. Ask clarifying questions: If you don't understand something the speaker said, ask for clarification. This demonstrates that you are genuinely interested in understanding their point of view.
5. Paraphrase: Repeat what the speaker said in your own words to ensure that you have understood their message correctly. This also shows that you are actively engaged and processing the information they are sharing.
6. Avoid distractions: Avoid distractions, such as background noise or other conversations, as they can interfere with your ability to actively listen.
7. Be patient: Active listening requires patience and an open mind. Avoid jumping to conclusions or making assumptions, as this can lead to misunderstandings.

By actively listening, you demonstrate that you value the speaker and their message. This skill is essential in building strong relationships, resolving conflicts, and effectively communicating in both personal and professional settings.

Using a Likert scale (1–5) or yes/no responses, rate yourself on each aspect of active listening listed above.

You can also ask colleagues or team members to rate you on the same aspects of active listening to gather a 360-degree view. The assessment results can help identify areas for improvement and provide insights for leadership development.

You might also want to think about these questions.

What gets in the way of you actively listening?

_____

_____

_____

_____

_____

How are you going to increase your active listening ability?

_____

_____

_____

_____

If you were to begin active listening what might be the ramifications?

_____

_____

_____

_____

Activity 6: Communication Style Assessment

This activity will help you identify your communication style. You will reflect on how you communicate with others and consider how this affects your leadership style and relationships with others.

INTRODUCTION

The way you communicate with others is an essential aspect of your life. Communication style refers to the way individuals interact with others through verbal and nonverbal means. Each person has a unique communication style that reflects their personality, cultural background, and life experiences.

ASSESSMENT

The following assessment is designed to help you identify your communication style. It consists of a series of questions that will evaluate how you typically communicate in different situations. Please answer each question honestly and choose the response that best reflects your usual communication behavior.

1. In a group setting, you prefer to:
   a) Listen and observe before speaking
   b) Jump in and contribute right away
2. When faced with a conflict, you tend to:
   a) Avoid confrontation and seek a compromise
   b) Address the issue directly and assertively
3. How do you usually express your emotions?
   a) Through body language and tone of voice
   b) Through explicit language and verbal communication
4. Do you prefer to communicate in a structured or unstructured manner?
   a) I prefer structured communication
   b) I prefer unstructured communication
5. In a conversation, do you tend to:
   a) Ask questions and actively listen
   b) Talk about yourself and your experiences
6. How do you typically handle criticism?

a) Listen to the feedback and try to understand the other person's perspective
b) Become defensive and explain why you disagree with the criticism

7. Do you prefer to communicate through written or verbal means?
a) I prefer written communication
b) I prefer verbal communication

8. How do you usually approach decision-making?
a) Consider multiple options and weigh the pros and cons
b) Trust your instincts and make a quick decision

9. How do you typically respond to feedback or suggestions?
a) Consider the feedback and evaluate whether it's useful or relevant
b) Dismiss the feedback and continue doing things your way

10. How do you typically convey your message to others?
a) Through storytelling and analogies
b) Through facts and logical reasoning

Scoring: To score your assessment, count the number of A and B responses you chose.

If you chose mostly A responses, you tend to have a more passive communication style. You are likely to listen before speaking, avoid confrontation, and consider others' perspectives before making decisions.

If you chose mostly B responses, you tend to have a more assertive communication style. You are likely to jump into conversations, address conflicts directly, and trust your instincts when making decisions.

Knowing your communication style can help you understand how you interact with others and improve your communication skills. By identifying your strengths and weaknesses, you can adapt your style to better connect with others and build stronger relationships.

What strengths and weaknesses that you identified in Part 1: Core awareness impact the way that you communicate?

What do you need to work on to increase your communication skills?

....

....

....

What is your preference for communication? Do you like people to be bold, direct, honest, and communicate via text? What are your personal communication needs? What are the personal communication needs of others?

....

....

....

Activity 7: Growth vs. Fixed Mindset

In her book *Mindset*, Carol Dweck takes a deep dive into a growth mindset vs. a fixed mindset. A growth mindset and fixed mindset are two different beliefs that individuals hold about their personal abilities and the way they view challenges and setbacks.

A fixed mindset refers to the belief that your personal traits, qualities, and abilities are static, unchangeable, and predetermined, and that failure is a sign of your limited abilities. People with a fixed mindset tend to avoid challenges, give up quickly when faced with obstacles, and feel threatened by the success of others. They also tend to ignore feedback and believe that talent alone is enough to succeed.

On the other hand, a growth mindset refers to the belief that your abilities, skills, and qualities can be developed through hard work, dedication, and learning. People with a growth mindset embrace challenges, persist in the face of obstacles, and see failure as an opportunity to learn and grow. They seek out feedback, are inspired by the success of others, and believe that with effort and time, they can improve in any area.

The following is a list of questions to consider to help determine if you have a growth or fixed mindset. Reflect on your personal beliefs about your abilities and how you handle challenges.

1. Do you believe that your abilities and intelligence are fixed traits that you can't change, or do you believe that you can improve with practice and effort?
2. How do you respond to setbacks and failures? Do you give up easily or see them as opportunities to learn and grow?
3. Do you avoid challenges that might expose your weaknesses, or do you embrace them as a chance to improve?
4. How do you feel about the success of others? Do you feel threatened by their achievements, or are you inspired to learn from them and strive to improve yourself?

By reflecting on these questions and examining your own beliefs, you can start to understand whether you have a growth or fixed mindset. It's important to remember that your mindset can change over time and with practice, and adopting a growth mindset, you can develop increased motivation, resilience, and success in all areas of life.

Activities that you can do to cultivate a growth mindset.

1. Encourage continuous learning: As a leader, you can promote a growth mindset by creating a culture of continuous learning and development. Encourage your team to take on new challenges, try new things, and take risks.
2. Provide opportunities for feedback: Feedback is essential for growth and improvement. Encourage your team to seek out feedback. Provide regular opportunities for critiquing through one-on-one meetings, performance evaluations, and team assessments.
3. Emphasize effort and process: Rather than focusing solely on results, emphasize the effort and process that went into achieving those results. Encourage your team to celebrate small wins along the way and to learn from failures.
4. Model a growth mindset: As a leader, you have a powerful influence on your team's mindset. Model a growth mindset by sharing your own learning experiences, being open to feedback, and embracing challenges and setbacks as opportunities for growth.
5. Provide resources for growth: Provide your team with resources and support to help them develop their skills and achieve their goals. This could include training programs, coaching, mentorship, or access to learning resources such as books, podcasts, and online courses.
6. Celebrate growth and improvement: Celebrate the progress and growth of your team members. Acknowledge their hard work, their successes, and the improvements they make over time.

7. Use growth mindset language: Language plays a critical role in shaping your mindset. Encourage your team to use growth mindset language by focusing on *effort, learning,* and *improvement* rather than *talent* or *fixed abilities.*

By incorporating these resources and activities into your leadership approach, you can help foster a growth mindset within your team and create a culture of continuous learning and improvement.

What behaviors do you need to implement, and put into practice, to cultivate a growth mindset?

....

....

....

....

....

Activity 8: Setting Expectations – 4-Step Process

1. Define expectations clearly. The first step for you is to define the expectations clearly. This means outlining specific goals, outcomes, behaviors, and metrics that the team members need to meet. Use simple language and avoid jargon to ensure that everyone understands what is expected of them.
2. Communicate expectations: Once the expectations are defined, it's important to communicate them effectively to the team members. Use multiple communication channels such as team meetings, emails, or one-on-one conversations to make sure everyone is on the same page.
3. Provide context and rationale: It's important to provide context and rationale behind the expectations to help team members understand the importance of meeting them. Explain how the expectations align with the team's goals, company values, or customer needs. This will motivate team members and help them see the 'bigger picture'.
4. Monitor progress and provide feedback: Finally, monitor the team's progress towards meeting the expectations and provide timely feedback. Use positive reinforcement for good performance and corrective feedback for areas that need improvement. Regularly review progress and adjust expectations if necessary to ensure they are realistic and achievable.

Using a Likert scale (1–5) or yes/no responses, rate yourself on each aspect of the 4-Step Process for Setting Clear Expectations listed above.

You can also ask colleagues or team members to rate you on the same aspects of the 4-Step Process for Setting Clear Expectations to gather a 360-degree view. The assessment results can help identify areas for improvement and provide insights for leadership development.

What part of the 4-Step Process for Setting Clear Expectations do you need to work on?

....

....

....

....

What is your plan of action based on what you have learned?

....

....

....

....

Activity 9: Feedback Exercise

This activity will help you develop your ability to give and receive feedback. You will practice giving constructive feedback to others and learn how to receive feedback in a way that promotes growth and improvement.

STRUCTURE FOR GIVING FEEDBACK

1. Start with a clear purpose: Before giving or receiving feedback, ensure that the purpose of the feedback is clear. The feedback should be focused on a specific task or behavior and should be designed to help the individual improve their performance.

2. Begin with positive feedback: Start by acknowledging what the individual did well. This can help build rapport and create a positive environment for receiving constructive criticism.

3. Provide specific feedback: Provide specific feedback on the task or behavior being discussed. Be clear, concise, and specific in your feedback. Use examples to illustrate your points and help the individual understand what you are referring to.

4. Focus on behavior, not personality: When giving feedback, focus on the behavior or task being discussed, rather than the individual's personality or character. This can help ensure that the feedback is constructive and not perceived as a personal attack.

5. Offer suggestions for improvement: After providing feedback, offer suggestions for how the individual can improve their performance. Be specific and offer actionable suggestions that the individual can implement.

6. Encourage dialogue: Encourage the individual to ask questions and seek clarification on the feedback. This can help ensure that the feedback is understood and can help the individual feel more comfortable receiving feedback in the future.

7. End on a positive note: End the feedback session on a positive note by reiterating what the individual did well and expressing confidence in their ability to improve. This can help leave the individual feeling motivated and encouraged to implement the feedback.

STRUCTURE FOR RECEIVING FEEDBACK

1. Listen actively: When someone gives you feedback, focus your attention on them and listen without interrupting. Try to understand their perspective and avoid getting defensive.

2. Clarify: Once the person has finished giving feedback, clarify any points that you didn't fully understand. Repeat back what you heard to ensure you understand the feedback accurately.

3. Express appreciation: Thank the person for giving you feedback. It takes courage to give feedback, and acknowledging this can help create a positive tone for the conversation.

4. Reflect: Take some time to reflect on the feedback. Consider the specific examples provided and try to see things from the person's perspective.

5. Consider action: Decide what action, if any, you will take in response to the feedback. Identify any changes you need to make, and if necessary, develop a plan to make those changes.

6. Follow up: If appropriate, follow up with the person who gave you feedback to let them know how you've responded to their feedback. This can help demonstrate your commitment to growth and improvement.

Remember, receiving feedback is an opportunity for growth and development. It can be difficult to hear criticism, but it's important to remain open-minded and receptive to feedback to learn from it.

When giving feedback, what do you need to focus on?

....

....

....

When receiving feedback what do you need to focus on?

....

....

....

In the next week, who do you need to give feedback to? In the next week, who do you need to ask for feedback?

....

....

....

Activity 10: Conflict Resolution Exercise

This activity will help you develop your conflict resolution skills. You will practice identifying and addressing conflicts in a productive and constructive way.

CONFLICT RESOLUTION ASSESSMENT

1. How do you typically respond when you encounter a conflict with someone else?
   a) I immediately become defensive and try to prove my point.
   b) I try to understand the other person's perspective and find common ground.
   c) I avoid the conflict and hope it will go away on its own.
   d) I become emotional and lash out at the other person.
2. How do you approach resolving a conflict with someone?
   a) I try to come up with a compromise that benefits both parties.
   b) I push my own agenda and try to get the other person to see things my way.
   c) I give in to the other person's demands to avoid further conflict.
   d) I refuse to engage in conflict resolution and instead escalate the situation.

3. How do you communicate during a conflict?
   a) I interrupt the other person and talk over them.
   b) I listen actively and try to understand their perspective.
   c) I become defensive and shut down communication.
   d) I resort to name-calling or other personal attacks.
4. How do you manage your emotions during a conflict?
   a) I take a break to cool off before continuing the conversation.
   b) I express my emotions in a constructive way to help the other person understand my point of view.
   c) I let my emotions control my behavior and escalate the conflict.
   d) I try to suppress my emotions and avoid addressing them.
5. How do you approach finding a resolution to the conflict?
   a) I brainstorm potential solutions with the other person.
   b) I dictate the terms of the resolution and expect the other person to comply.
   c) I give in to the other person's demands to end the conflict quickly.
   d) I refuse to compromise and hold out for my own solution.

Scoring: For questions 1–5, give yourself one point for every (b) answer, and subtract one point for every (a), (c), or (d) answer. The maximum possible score is five, and the minimum possible score is -5.

Interpretation: A score of 4 or 5 indicates that you have strong conflict resolution skills and are likely able to resolve conflicts effectively. A score of 0 to 3 indicates that there is room for improvement in your conflict resolution skills, and you may benefit from further training or practice. A score of -1 to -5 indicates that you may have significant difficulty resolving conflicts and may need more intensive intervention or counseling to improve your skills.

What did you learn about your conflict style?

....

....

....

....

....

STRUCTURE TO RESOLVE CONFLICT

1. Take a moment to calm down: Conflict can be emotional, and it's important to take a moment to calm down before trying to resolve it. Take deep breaths or engage in a calming activity like taking a walk or listening to music.

2. Identify the issue: Clearly identify the issue at hand and what specifically caused the conflict. This will help you stay focused on the issue and prevent the conversation from spiraling out of control.

3. Listen actively: Listen carefully to the other person's perspective and try to understand their point of view. Ask questions to clarify their position and avoid making assumptions.

4. Express your own perspective: Share your own thoughts and feelings about the situation. Use "I" statements to avoid blaming or accusing the other person.

5. Brainstorm solutions: Work together to come up with potential solutions to the conflict. Be open to compromise and consider the other person's needs and wants.

6. Choose a solution: Evaluate the potential solutions and choose the one that works best for both parties. Make sure the solution is practical and realistic.

7. Follow up: Once a solution has been chosen, follow up with the other person to make sure it's working. If it's not, revisit the issue and try to come up with a new solution.

Remember, resolving conflict takes practice and patience. Be willing to listen, compromise, and work together to find a solution that works for everyone involved.

What is your action plan for resolving conflict? What do you need to be accountable for?

Activity 11: Control, Influence, Concern

You can link control, influence, and concern to the colors green, yellow, and red, respectively.

Green can represent control because it symbolizes growth, stability, and harmony. When you have control over a situation, you can cultivate a sense of growth and stability, and create a harmonious environment where things run smoothly.

Yellow can represent influence because it symbolizes energy, optimism, and creativity. When you have influence, you can use your energy, optimism, and creativity to inspire others and shape their attitudes and behaviors towards a particular outcome.

Red can represent concern because it symbolizes passion, intensity, and urgency. When you are deeply concerned about something, you feel a sense of passion and intensity, and you may be motivated to take urgent action to ensure its success.

By using these colors to represent control, influence, and concern, you can create a visual shorthand for understanding and communicating these concepts. For example, if you are discussing a project and someone mentions that they have a lot of control over the outcome, you might visualize this as a green light, indicating that things are under control and moving forward smoothly. If someone else mentions that they are concerned about a particular aspect of the project, you might visualize this as a red light, indicating that urgent action may be needed to address the issue. And if someone else mentions that they are using their influence to motivate others towards a particular outcome, you might visualize this as a yellow light, indicating that they are using their energy and creativity to inspire others.

What is your action plan for moving forward? What do you need to be accountable for and what is in your circle of control? What do you need to let go of?

....

....

....

....

....

....

Activity 12: Limiting Beliefs

Limiting beliefs are negative thoughts and ideas that you hold about yourself and the world around you. These beliefs can hold you back from achieving your goals, limit your potential, and prevent you from taking action towards success. Limiting beliefs can come from a variety of sources, such as past experiences, cultural conditioning, and societal expectations.

In the context of accountability, limiting beliefs can be a significant obstacle to achieving your desired outcomes. When you hold negative beliefs about yourself and your abilities, you are less likely to take responsibility for your actions and take steps towards achieving your goals. You may fall into a pattern of making excuses, blaming others, or avoiding difficult tasks. However, by identifying and challenging your limiting beliefs, you can develop a more positive and growth-oriented mindset that allows you to take ownership of your actions and make progress toward your goals. By taking accountability for your actions, you can overcome limiting beliefs and achieve success in all areas of your life.

ASSESSMENT

1. Write down a goal or desire that you have been wanting to achieve but have been struggling with.
2. Make a list of any beliefs or thoughts that come up when you think about achieving that goal. These could be thoughts such as "I'm not good enough," "I don't have the skills," "I don't have enough time," etc.
3. For each belief or thought, ask yourself the following questions:
   - Is this belief true?
   - Is there any evidence that contradicts this belief?
   - How does this belief limit me in achieving my goal?

- What would happen if I didn't have this belief?

EXERCISE

1. Choose one of the limiting beliefs you identified in the assessment.
2. Write down a statement that contradicts that belief. For example, if your belief is "I'm not good enough," your statement could be "I am capable and worthy of achieving my goals."
3. Repeat this statement to yourself several times a day, preferably in front of a mirror.
4. Whenever the limiting belief comes up, consciously replace it with the new statement. This will help retrain your brain to think in a more positive and empowering way.
5. Take action towards your goal, even if it's just a small step. This will help you build confidence and prove to yourself that the limiting belief is not true.

Repeat this exercise with each of the limiting beliefs you identified in the assessment. Over time, you will begin to notice a shift in your thinking and behavior, and you will be more equipped to achieve your goals.

Part 2: Core Behaviors Review

What have I learned and put into practice in Part 2: Core Behaviors?

....

....

....

....

....

What have I learned that I could do differently because of Part 2: Core Behaviors?

....

....

....

....

....

What will be my next steps? What can I start, stop, and continue to do?

"THE GREATEST LEADER IS NOT NECESSARILY THE ONE WHO DOES THE GREATEST THINGS. HE IS THE ONE THAT GETS THE PEOPLE TO DO THE GREATEST THINGS."

–PRESIDENT RONALD REAGAN

Part 3: Core Connections

Activity 13: Vision

Activity 14: Collaboration

Activity 15: Energy and Time

Activity 16: Best Self/Worst Self

Activity 17: Trust

Activity 18: Accountability

Activity 19: Power, Influence & Negotiation

Activity 20: Team Leadership & Assessment

Activity 13: Vision Exercise

This activity will help you develop your ability to create a compelling vision for your team or organization. You will reflect on your own vision for the future and learn how to communicate this vision to others. Clarity of focus leads to accuracy of response. If you get clear on your vision, then you and others will know how to respond appropriately.

Overview on Vision: Vision refers to a clear and compelling picture of the future that inspires and motivates individuals and organizations to achieve their goals. It provides a sense of direction and purpose, helps to align actions with values, and enables individuals to overcome obstacles and challenges. As a leader, having a clear vision can help you to inspire and motivate your team, to make strategic decisions, and to create a roadmap for success.

Activity: To develop a clearer vision as a leader, try the following activity.

1. Reflect on your values and goals: Take some time to reflect on your personal values and the goals you want to achieve as a leader. Write them down and consider how they align with your organization's mission and values.

2. Imagine the future: Imagine yourself in the future, say 5–10 years from now. What do you want your organization to look like? What kind of impact do you want to make? What are your goals and objectives? Write down your ideas and be as specific as possible.

3. Create a vision statement: Based on your reflections and imaginings, create a vision statement that captures the essence of your vision for the future. Your vision statement should be concise, clear, and inspiring. Make sure it aligns with your values and goals.

4. Share your vision: Share your vision statement with your team and get their feedback. Encourage them to share their own ideas and visions for the future. Use their feedback to refine your vision statement and ensure it resonates with your team.

5. Align actions with vision: Once you have a clear vision, it's important to align your actions with that vision. Use your vision statement as a guide for decision-making and goal-setting. Communicate your vision to your team and ensure that everyone is working towards the same goals. Regularly review and update your vision to ensure it remains relevant and inspiring.

What is your vision? What will your next steps be for action?

....

....

....

....

....

Activity 14: Collaboration

Collaborating with others from different departments is essential for achieving organizational success. In today's complex and interconnected business environment, no department or individual can operate in isolation. Each department brings unique skills, knowledge, and perspectives that are essential to achieving the organization's goals. By working together, cross-functional teams can leverage their diverse strengths to develop innovative solutions, increase efficiency, and achieve better outcomes than any department could achieve alone.

Effective collaboration also helps to break down silos and promote a culture of teamwork and shared responsibility. When colleagues from different departments work together, they gain a better understanding of each other's roles and challenges, which fosters mutual respect and builds trust. This can help to reduce conflicts and misunderstandings, improve communication and decision-making, and promote a sense of shared ownership over the organization's success. In addition, when employees feel valued and connected to their colleagues across departments, they are more likely to feel engaged, motivated, and committed to the organization's mission and goals. Ultimately, by fostering a collaborative culture that encourages cross-functional teamwork, organizations can build stronger relationships, achieve better results, and create a more resilient and adaptable workforce.

ASSESSMENT: COLLABORATING WITH CROSS-FUNCTIONAL TEAMS

Instructions: This assessment is designed to help you evaluate your ability to work effectively with colleagues from different departments and job functions within your organization.

Score	Rate yourself on the following statements using a scale of 1–5, where 1 is "strongly disagree" and 5 is "strongly agree."
	I actively seek out opportunities to collaborate with colleagues from other departments.
	I make an effort to understand the perspectives and goals of colleagues from other departments.
	I am able to communicate clearly and effectively with colleagues from other departments.
	I am comfortable delegating tasks to colleagues from other departments.
	I am open to feedback and suggestions from colleagues from other departments.
	I recognize and appreciate the unique skills and expertise that colleagues from other departments bring to the table.
	I am able to negotiate effectively with colleagues from other departments to reach mutually beneficial outcomes.
	I make an effort to build strong relationships with colleagues from other departments.
	I am able to adapt my communication and leadership style to suit the needs of different departments and job functions.
	I am able to prioritize competing demands and needs from different departments and job functions.

Scoring

- Add up your scores for each statement.
- A score of 40–50 indicates that you are a highly effective collaborator who is able to work well with colleagues from different departments and job functions.
- A score of 30–39 indicates that you have some strengths in collaborating with cross-functional teams, but there is room for improvement.
- A score of 20–29 indicates that you may need to work on your ability to collaborate effectively with colleagues from different departments and job functions.
- A score below 20 indicates that you may struggle with collaborating with others from different departments and job functions and could benefit from further development.

Interpreting Your Results

- Review your responses to the individual statements to identify areas where you feel particularly strong or where you could improve.
- Consider seeking feedback from colleagues in different departments to gain additional insights into your strengths and areas for improvement.
- Use your results to develop an action plan for how you can become a better business partner and collaborate more effectively with colleagues from different departments and job functions.

What do you plan on doing with this information? What is your course of action and next steps?

....

....

....

....

....

....

Activity 15: Energy and Time

Time, energy, and being overwhelmed are all interconnected concepts that can significantly impact your daily life. When you have a limited amount of time to complete a long list of tasks, it can be challenging to maintain high energy levels and avoid feeling overwhelmed.

One of the biggest contributors to feeling overwhelmed is the inability to manage your time effectively. When you have too much to do in a limited amount of time, you may end up procrastinating, multitasking, or trying to do too much at once. These behaviors can quickly drain your energy levels and make you feel even more overwhelmed.

Another factor that can impact your energy levels and contribute to feelings of overwhelm is stress. When you are stressed, your body releases cortisol, a hormone that can lead to fatigue and decreased energy levels over time. Chronic stress can also impact your sleep patterns, making it more difficult to get the rest you need to maintain high energy levels.

To avoid feeling overwhelmed, it's essential to manage your time and energy levels effectively. One way to do this is by practicing good time management habits, such as prioritizing tasks, setting realistic goals, and breaking down larger projects into smaller, more manageable tasks. It's also essential to establish healthy habits that can help us maintain high energy levels, such as getting enough sleep, eating a balanced diet, staying hydrated, and engaging in regular physical exercise.

If you're feeling overwhelmed, taking a break can also be helpful. Stepping away from a task or project for a few minutes can help you recharge and come back to it with renewed energy and focus. It's also important to practice self-care, such as mindfulness or meditation, which can help you manage stress and maintain a sense of balance and calm.

Time, energy, and being overwhelmed are all interconnected concepts that require effective management to ensure that you can achieve your goals and maintain a sense of well-being. By prioritizing tasks, practicing healthy habits, and taking breaks when necessary, you can manage your time and energy levels effectively, avoid feelings of overwhelm, and achieve your desired outcomes.

TIME MANAGEMENT ASSESSMENT YOU CAN USE TO EVALUATE YOUR CURRENT TIME MANAGEMENT HABITS

1. Do you use a daily planner or schedule to plan your day?
   a) Yes, I plan my day in advance using a planner or schedule.
   b) No, I don't use a planner or schedule to plan my day.
2. Do you prioritize your tasks and activities?
   a) Yes, I prioritize my tasks and activities based on their importance and urgency.
   b) No, I don't prioritize my tasks and activities.
3. How often do you get distracted while working?
   a) Rarely, I'm able to stay focused on my work most of the time.
   b) Occasionally, I get distracted but I'm able to refocus quickly.
   c) Frequently, I find myself getting distracted and have difficulty refocusing.
4. How often do you multitask?
   a) Rarely, I focus on one task at a time.
   b) Occasionally, I may switch between tasks, but I stay focused on each task.
   c) Frequently, I try to work on multiple tasks simultaneously.
5. Do you take breaks during the day?
   a) Yes, I take breaks periodically to rest and recharge.
   b) No, I work through the day without taking any breaks.

6. How often do you check your email and social media during the day?
   a) Rarely, I check my email and social media only when I have free time.
   b) Occasionally, I check my email and social media a few times during the day.
   c) Frequently, I check my email and social media multiple times throughout the day.
7. Do you delegate tasks to others when appropriate?
   a) Yes, I delegate tasks to others when it makes sense to do so.
   b) No, I prefer to do everything myself.
8. How often do you evaluate your time management habits?
   a) Regularly, I evaluate my time management habits and make changes when necessary.
   b) Infrequently, I rarely evaluate my time management habits.

Scoring: For questions 1–7, give yourself one point for each (a) answer and zero points for each (b) or (c) answer. For question 8, give yourself two points for an (a) answer and one point for a (b) answer.

Interpretation: 8–10 points: Your time management skills are excellent! You have effective habits in place to manage your time and accomplish your tasks efficiently. 5–7 points: Your time management skills could use some improvement. There are areas where you can make changes to be more productive and effective. 0–4 points: Your time management skills need significant improvement. You may benefit from working with a coach or mentor to develop better habits and strategies for managing your time.

STRATEGIES THAT CAN HELP YOU PRIORITIZE AND USE YOUR TIME MORE EFFECTIVELY

1. Time blocking: This involves breaking up your day into blocks of time and dedicating each block to a specific task or activity. This helps you stay focused and avoid multitasking.
2. To-do lists: Make a list of tasks you need to accomplish and prioritize them according to their importance and urgency. This will help you stay organized and focused on the most important tasks.
3. Eisenhower Matrix: This is a tool that helps you categorize tasks into four categories: Urgent and important, important but not urgent, urgent but not important, and neither urgent nor important. This helps you prioritize tasks and focus on the most important ones first.
4. Pomodoro Technique: This technique involves breaking up your workday into 25-minute intervals, with a 5-minute break in between each interval. After four intervals, take a longer break of 20–30 minutes. This helps you stay focused and avoid burnout.
5. Time-tracking apps: There are many time-tracking apps available that help you keep track of how much time you spend on each task. This helps you identify time wasters and become more efficient.

6. Say no: Learning to say no to tasks and requests that are not important or urgent can help you free up more time to focus on the things that matter most.

7. Delegate: If you have tasks that can be done by someone else, consider delegating them. This will help you free up more time and focus on the tasks that require your attention.

8. Batch similar tasks: If you have tasks that are similar in nature, consider batching them together. This can help you save time and be more efficient.

9. Use the 80/20 rule: The 80/20 rule states that 80% of your results come from 20% of your efforts. Identify the tasks that are most important and focus on them first.

10. Set goals: Setting clear and specific goals can help you prioritize your time and stay focused on what matters most. It also gives you a sense of purpose and direction.

What will be your next steps? How will you evaluate and measure success?

....

....

....

....

Activity 16: Best Self/Worst Self

BEST SELF/WORST SELF ACTIVITY

1. Find a quiet and comfortable place where you won't be disturbed.

2. Take out a piece of paper and divide it into two columns - one for "Best Self" and the other for "Worst Self."

3. In the "Best Self" column, write down all the positive traits, values, and characteristics that you believe describe you at your best. Some examples might include: compassionate, honest, ambitious, resilient, creative, etc. Think about your strengths and what makes you feel proud of yourself.

4. In the "Worst Self" column, write down all the negative traits, habits, and behaviors that you recognize in yourself when you are not at your best. Some examples might include: selfish, lazy, impulsive, dishonest, insecure, etc. Think about what you are ashamed of and what you would like to change.

5. Take a moment to reflect on each item on your list. What situations or circumstances tend to bring out your best or worst self? Are there any patterns or common themes that you notice?

6. Finally, think about what actions you can take to cultivate your best self and minimize your worst self. Consider setting specific goals or making changes to your environment or routine to support your growth.

Remember, this activity is not meant to judge or criticize yourself. It's an opportunity to be honest with yourself and gain insights into your own behavior and mindset. By identifying your best and worst self, you can start to make conscious choices that align with your values and lead to a more fulfilling life.

Identifying your best self and worst self can help you build stronger and more authentic connections with others. Here are a few ways this can happen.

1. Increased self-awareness: By reflecting on your positive and negative traits, you gain a better understanding of how you show up in relationships. This self-awareness can help you recognize patterns in your behavior, identify triggers for your worst self, and make conscious choices to bring out your best self.

2. Improved communication: When you know your own strengths and weaknesses, you can communicate more effectively with others. For example, you can express your needs and boundaries clearly, ask for help when you need it, and apologize and make amends when you make a mistake.

3. Deeper connections: When you are able to show up as your best self, you are more likely to attract and maintain positive relationships. People are naturally drawn to those who are kind, compassionate, and authentic. By cultivating these traits in yourself, you can build deeper and more meaningful connections with others.

4. Resilience: Knowing your worst self can help you better handle conflict and challenges in your relationships. When you understand your triggers and tendencies, you can prepare yourself to respond in a more constructive way. This resilience can help you navigate difficult situations and maintain stronger connections with others over time.

Identifying your best self and worst self can help you build more fulfilling relationships with others. By understanding your own strengths and weaknesses, you can communicate more effectively, cultivate deeper connections, and navigate challenges with greater resilience.

USE THE SPACE BELOW TO COMPLETE THE ABOVE ACTIVITY

Best Self	Worst Self

Activity 17: Trust

Trust is an essential component of effective connections with others and for teams to function at their highest potential. Without trust, individuals and teams struggle to build strong relationships, communicate effectively, and work collaboratively towards shared goals. When trust is absent, people tend to be guarded, defensive, and hesitant to share their thoughts and feelings. This can lead to misunderstandings, conflicts, and a lack of productivity.

On the other hand, when trust is present, individuals and teams are able to work together more cohesively and effectively. Trust creates an environment of safety, where people feel comfortable sharing their opinions, making mistakes, and taking risks. It allows individuals to rely on each other and to have confidence that their colleagues will follow through on their commitments. This leads to increased cooperation, better communication, and a stronger sense of unity within the team.

In addition, trust is also essential for creating a positive work culture. When people trust each other, they tend to feel more engaged and satisfied in their work. They are more likely to feel supported, valued, and respected, which can lead to increased motivation and productivity. Overall, trust is a critical ingredient for building effective connections with others and for teams to thrive, and it requires ongoing effort and commitment to maintain.

Stephen Covey has identified 13 trust building behaviors that are important to know for meaningful connections.

Stephen Covey's 13 trust-building behaviors are outlined in his book "The Speed of Trust" and are designed to help individuals build trust in personal and professional relationships. These behaviors are:

1. Talk straight: Be honest and tell the truth in all situations.
2. Demonstrate respect: Treat others with kindness, courtesy, and consideration.
3. Create transparency: Be open and upfront about your intentions, decisions, and actions.
4. Right wrongs: Take responsibility for your mistakes and make amends when necessary.
5. Show loyalty: Stand by your commitments and be loyal to those who are not present.
6. Deliver results: Follow through on your promises and consistently deliver high-quality work.
7. Get better: Continuously learn and improve your skills and abilities.
8. Confront reality: Face difficult situations and have the courage to address them.
9. Clarify expectations: Make sure everyone understands their roles, responsibilities, and expectations.
10. Practice accountability: Hold yourself and others accountable for their actions and results.
11. Listen first: Seek to understand before being understood.
12. Keep commitments: Do what you say you will do and follow through on your promises.
13. Extend trust: Be willing to trust others and give them the benefit of the doubt.

ASSESSMENT

Below is an assessment designed to help you evaluate your level of proficiency in each of the 13 trust-building behaviors. For each behavior, rate yourself on a scale of 1–5. 1 - Never or almost never do this 2 - Seldom do this 3 - Sometimes do this 4 - Often do this 5 - Always or almost always do this.

Talk straight:	
Demonstrate respect:	
Create transparency:	
Right wrongs:	
Show loyalty:	
Deliver results:	
Get better:	
Confront reality:	
Clarify expectations:	
Practice accountability:	
Listen first:	
Keep commitments:	
Extend trust:	

Once you have completed the assessment, review your responses and identify the behaviors where you scored the lowest. Consider why these behaviors are challenging for you and what steps you can take to improve in these areas. Use the assessment as a tool to help you become more aware of your strengths and weaknesses when it comes to building trust with others.

What Trust Building behaviors do you need to work on? What will be your next steps?

....

....

....

....

....

Activity 18: Accountability

Accountability is a crucial aspect of completing tasks effectively, both as an individual and as part of a team. It refers to taking responsibility for one's actions and ensuring that commitments are fulfilled in a timely and satisfactory manner. In the context of task completion, accountability involves being proactive, keeping track of deadlines, and communicating regularly with others involved in the project.

Assessment: Accountability is essential for effective connections and task completion in several ways:

1. Responsibility: Being accountable means taking ownership of tasks and assignments. It is a commitment to delivering on what you promised, and being responsible for the outcome. When you hold yourself accountable, you are more likely to take initiative and ensure that tasks are completed to the best of their abilities.

2. Time Management: Effective task completion often depends on proper time management. Being accountable means setting realistic deadlines, prioritizing tasks, and staying focused on the goal. When you are accountable for your time, you are less likely to procrastinate or become distracted by other tasks.

3. Communication: Accountability also involves communicating regularly with others involved in the project. This includes providing updates on progress, identifying any challenges or obstacles, and seeking feedback from others. Effective communication helps to build trust, foster collaboration, and ensure that everyone is working towards the same goals.

4. Consequences: Holding oneself accountable also means accepting the consequences of one's actions. This includes acknowledging mistakes and taking steps to rectify them. When you are accountable you are more likely to learn from your mistakes and grow from the experience.

ACCOUNTABILITY ASSESSMENT TO EVALUATE ACCOUNTABILITY FOR TASKS AND RELATIONSHIPS

PART 1: ACCOUNTABILITY FOR TASKS

1. How often do you set clear goals and deadlines for your tasks?
   a) Almost always
   b) Sometimes
   c) Rarely
   d) Never

2. When faced with unexpected obstacles, how do you respond?
   a) Immediately communicate with team members and develop a plan to address the obstacle
   b) Try to handle it on my own and hope for the best
   c) Ignore it and hope it goes away
   d) Blame others for the obstacle

3. How do you manage your time when completing tasks?
   a) Use a task management system or tool to stay organized
   b) Write down tasks on a to-do list and prioritize based on importance
   c) Tend to procrastinate until the last minute
   d) Struggle to manage time and often miss deadlines

4. When you miss a deadline or fail to complete a task, how do you respond?
   a) Immediately take responsibility for the mistake and work to fix it
   b) Blame external factors for the failure
   c) Ignore the situation and hope it goes unnoticed
   d) Blame other team members for the failure

5. How often do you provide updates on your progress to team members?
   a) Regularly, at least once a week
   b) Occasionally, when asked
   c) Rarely, only when prompted
   d) Never, I assume everyone knows what I'm working on

PART 2: ACCOUNTABILITY FOR RELATIONSHIPS

1. How often do you take responsibility for misunderstandings or conflicts in a relationship?
   a) Almost always
   b) Sometimes
   c) Rarely
   d) Never

2. When a relationship becomes strained, how do you attempt to repair it?
   a) Apologize and work towards a resolution
   b) Avoid confrontation and hope it resolves on its own
   c) Blame the other person for the problem
   d) Ignore the issue and hope it goes away

3. How do you communicate your needs and expectations in a relationship?
   a) Clearly and respectfully
   b) Vaguely and indirectly
   c) Avoid communicating my needs and expectations
   d) Expect the other person to read my mind

4. How do you respond when someone expresses dissatisfaction with your behavior in a relationship?
   a) Listen to their feedback and work to improve
   b) Dismiss their feedback and continue the behavior
   c) Become defensive and argue with the person
   d) Blame the other person for the problem

5. How often do you show appreciation and gratitude towards the people in your relationships?
   a) Regularly, at least once a week
   b) Occasionally, when the opportunity arises
   c) Rarely, only when prompted
   d) Never, I assume people know that I appreciate them

Scoring: For each question, give yourself the following points: a) 3 points b) 2 points c) 1 point d) 0 points.

Add up your scores for Part 1 and Part 2 separately, then use the following key to interpret your results.

18-25: You are highly accountable for both tasks and relationships. You take responsibility for your actions, communicate effectively, and work to improve yourself and your relationships.

12-17: You are moderately accountable for tasks and relationships. While you are generally responsible, there may be areas where you could improve your communication or take more initiative.

6-11: You are minimally accountable for tasks and relationships. You may struggle with time management, communication, or taking responsibility for your actions.

0-5: You are not very accountable for tasks and relationships. You may frequently miss deadlines, blame others for problems, or have strained relationships due to lack of accountability.

The RACI model is a widely used framework for defining and communicating roles and responsibilities within an organization or project. The acronym RACI stands for Responsible, Accountable, Consulted, and Informed, which are the four key roles involved in any task or project.

- Responsible: This role is responsible for carrying out the task or completing the work. They are the "doers" who are responsible for making sure the task is completed on time and to the required standard.
- Accountable: This role is ultimately responsible for the task or project's success. They are the "decision-makers" who are accountable for ensuring that the task is completed to the required standard and within the agreed timeline.
- Consulted: This role is required to provide input or expertise to the task or project. They are the "advisors" who are consulted to provide information or guidance to ensure that the task is completed to the required standard.
- Informed: This role is kept informed of the task or project's progress. They are the "stakeholders" who need to be informed about the task's progress but do not have any decision-making authority.

Using the RACI model helps to clarify roles and responsibilities within a team or project, reducing confusion and ensuring that everyone knows what they are responsible for. It can also help to identify any gaps or overlaps in responsibilities, which can be addressed before they become problems.

To use the RACI model, you start by defining the task or project and identifying the key stakeholders involved. Then, you assign each stakeholder a RACI role based on their involvement in the task. It's important to communicate these roles and responsibilities clearly to everyone involved in the project to avoid any confusion or misunderstandings.

The RACI model is a valuable tool for improving accountability and communication within an organization or project team, ensuring that everyone knows what is expected of them and helping to ensure the successful completion of tasks and projects.

What did you learn about yourself as it relates to accountability? Are you accountable for both tasks and relationships? If not, what is getting in the way?

....

....

....

....

Activity 19: Power, Influence & Negotiation

Power, influence, and negotiation are important concepts for you to understand as they are essential to effective leadership. Power refers to the ability to get things done, influence is the ability to persuade others, and negotiation is the ability to reach agreements. Here's an overview of these concepts and how you can assess yourself in each area.

1. Power: Power is the ability to get things done, to make things happen. It can come from various sources, such as one's position within an organization or their expertise and knowledge. A leader with power can use it to influence people, make decisions, and drive change.
    ASSESSING YOUR POWER.
    - Identify your sources of power. What gives you power within your organization or team?
    - Evaluate how you use your power. Are you using it ethically and responsibly?
    - Assess how effective your power is. Are you getting things done? Are people following your lead?

2. Influence: Influence is the ability to persuade others to change their behavior or beliefs. A leader with influence can inspire people, motivate them to take action, and achieve goals.
    ASSESSING YOUR INFLUENCE.
    - Evaluate your communication skills. Are you able to articulate your ideas effectively?
    - Assess how you connect with others. Do people listen to you? Do you have credibility?
    - Evaluate how you inspire people. Are you able to motivate others to take action?

3. Negotiation: Negotiation is the ability to reach agreements with others. A leader who is skilled at negotiation can resolve conflicts, reach compromises, and make deals that benefit everyone involved.
    ASSESSING YOUR NEGOTIATION SKILLS.
    - Evaluate your communication skills. Are you able to listen actively and ask questions?
    - Assess your ability to collaborate. Can you work with others to find common ground?
    - Evaluate your problem-solving skills. Can you identify solutions that benefit all parties involved?

Understanding power, influence, and negotiation is critical for you to be an effective leader. By assessing yourself in each area, you can identify your strengths and weaknesses and develop strategies to improve your leadership skills.

In order to increase power, influence, and negotiation skills, it is important to understand the principles and techniques that underpin these skills. Here are some examples and tools for how to increase power, influence, and negotiation skills.

1. Building Power
    a) Positional Power: This type of power is derived from one's formal position or role in an organization. For example, a CEO or manager has positional power.
    b) Personal Power: This type of power is derived from one's personal characteristics, such as charisma, expertise, or reputation. For example, a well-known author or public speaker has personal power.
    SOME TOOLS AND STRATEGIES TO INCREASE POWER INCLUDE:
        i. Networking: Building relationships with influential people within an organization or industry can help to increase one's power.
        ii. Building expertise: Developing specialized knowledge or skills in a particular area can enhance one's personal power.
        iii. Building a reputation: Developing a positive reputation for integrity, reliability, and competence can increase personal power.
2. Building Influence
    a) Social Influence: This type of influence refers to the power to shape the attitudes or behaviors of others through social interaction. For example, a celebrity endorsing a product can influence people's attitudes towards it.
    b) Expert Influence: This type of influence is based on the perception that one has specialized knowledge or expertise in a particular area. For example, a doctor's recommendation can influence a patient's decision to take a particular medication.
    SOME TOOLS AND STRATEGIES TO INCREASE INFLUENCE INCLUDE:
        i. Building rapport: Establishing a positive connection with others can enhance one's social influence.
        ii. Building expertise: Developing specialized knowledge or skills in a particular area can enhance expert influence.
        iii. Providing value: Sharing valuable information or resources with others can increase one's influence.

3. Building Negotiation Skills

Negotiation skills involve the ability to communicate effectively, understand the other party's perspective, and reach a mutually beneficial agreement. Some tools and strategies to increase negotiation skills include:

a) Preparation: Conducting research, clarifying goals, and anticipating potential objections can enhance negotiation skills.

b) Active listening: Listening carefully to the other party's needs and concerns can help to build rapport and identify opportunities for compromise.

c) Flexibility: Being willing to explore different options and adapt to changing circumstances can increase the likelihood of reaching a mutually beneficial agreement.

d) Communication: Effective communication skills, such as clear articulation of one's needs and active listening to the other party, are essential for successful negotiation.

SOME TOOLS AND RESOURCES TO HELP INCREASE POWER, INFLUENCE, AND NEGOTIATION SKILLS INCLUDE:

- **Books**: "Influence: The Psychology of Persuasion" by Robert Cialdini, "Getting to Yes: Negotiating Agreement Without Giving In" by Roger Fisher and William Ury, "Power: Why Some People Have It and Others Don't" by Jeffrey Pfeffer.

- **Online Courses**: Coursera offers courses on Power, Influence, and Negotiation from top universities such as Duke University and the University of Michigan.

- **Workshops and Conferences**: Attending conferences and workshops focused on power, influence, and negotiation can provide opportunities to network, learn from experts, and practice skills in a supportive environment.

- **Mentors and Coaches**: Working with a mentor or coach who has expertise in power, influence, and negotiation can provide personalized feedback and guidance to help develop these skills.

ASSESSMENT POWER, INFLUENCE, AND NEGOTIATION

POWER ASSESSMENT

a) On a scale of 1–10, rate your ability to exert power or authority in a situation.

b) How comfortable are you with using power to influence others?

c) Give an example of a situation where you effectively used your power or authority to achieve a desired outcome.

INFLUENCE ASSESSMENT

a) On a scale of 1–10, rate your ability to influence others without using formal power or authority.

b) What techniques do you typically use to influence others?

c) Give an example of a situation where you successfully influenced others without using formal power or authority.

NEGOTIATION ASSESSMENT

a) On a scale of 1–10, rate your ability to negotiate effectively.

b) What negotiation techniques do you typically use?

c) Give an example of a negotiation you were involved in where you achieved a favorable outcome.

OVERALL ASSESSMENT

a) On a scale of 1–10, rate your overall ability to manage power, influence, and negotiation in various situations.

b) What areas do you feel you need to improve in?

c) What steps can you take to improve your skills in power, influence, and negotiation?

Note: These questions are just a starting point for you to assess your skills in power, influence, and negotiation.

What area do you need to work on: Power, Influence or Negotiation?

....

....

....

....

....

....

....

Activity 20: Team Leadership – Assessment

To be an effective leader of a team, there are a few key things that you should keep in mind. Here are some tips.

1. Set clear expectations: As a leader, it's important to clearly communicate what you expect from your team. This includes setting clear goals and outlining how you want those goals to be achieved.

2. Build trust: Trust is an essential component of any successful team. As a leader, you need to demonstrate that you trust your team members and that you're willing to listen to their ideas and feedback.

3. Communicate effectively: Effective communication is essential for any team to function well. Make sure you're clear and concise in your communication, and that you listen actively to what your team members are saying.

4. Encourage collaboration: Encourage your team members to work together and share their ideas. This can help to foster creativity and innovation within the team.

5. Provide feedback: Regular feedback is essential for team members to improve and grow. Make sure you're providing both positive feedback for things that are going well, as well as constructive feedback to help your team members improve.

6. Lead by example: As a leader, you need to set an example for your team. This means demonstrating the behavior and values that you expect from your team members.

On a scale from 1–5 with 1 being low and 5 being high, rate yourself on the above behaviors.

What do you need to focus on moving forward and what will you plan on doing this week?

....

....

....

....

Below are some questions to consider for you and your team on a weekly basis.

1. Do you set clear expectations for your team members?
2. Do you build trust with your team members?
3. Do you communicate effectively with your team?
4. Do you encourage collaboration among your team members?
5. Do you provide regular feedback to your team members?
6. Do you lead by example and demonstrate the behavior and values that you expect from your team members?

By answering these questions honestly, you can gain insights into your strengths as a leader, as well as areas where you may need to improve.

LEADERSHIP ASSESSMENT

For each question, rate yourself on a scale of 1–5, with 1 being "strongly disagree" and 5 being "strongly agree". Then, add up your scores for each category and divide by the number of questions in that category to get an average score. Finally, add up all seven average scores and divide by seven to get your overall score.

1. Visionary Thinking
   - Do you have a clear vision for your organization or team?
   - Are you able to communicate your vision to others effectively?
   - Do you regularly assess your vision and make necessary adjustments?
2. Communication
   - Are you a good listener?
   - Do you communicate effectively and clearly?
   - Are you approachable and open to feedback?
3. Decision Making
   - Are you able to make timely and effective decisions?
   - Do you involve others in the decision-making process when appropriate?
   - Do you weigh the potential risks and benefits before making a decision?
4. Motivation
   - Are you able to motivate and inspire your team?
   - Do you recognize and reward team members for their hard work and achievements?
   - Do you provide opportunities for growth and development?
5. Collaboration
   - Do you promote collaboration and teamwork?
   - Do you encourage open communication and constructive feedback?
   - Do you seek input from diverse perspectives before making decisions?
6. Adaptability
   - Are you able to adapt to changing circumstances and priorities?
   - Do you embrace new ideas and approaches?
   - Do you learn from failure and use it as an opportunity for growth?
7. Integrity
   - Do you act with honesty and integrity in all situations?
   - Do you hold yourself and others accountable for their actions?
   - Do you treat others with respect and fairness?

Interpretation

4.0 or above: Exceptional leadership skills

3.5–3.9: Good leadership skills, with room for improvement

3.0–3.4: Average leadership skills, needs improvement

Below 3.0: Poor leadership skills, requires significant improvement

Part 3: Core Connections Review

What have I learned and put into practice in Part 3: Core Connections?

_____

_____

_____

_____

_____

What have I learned that I could do differently because of Part 3: Core Connections?

_____

_____

_____

_____

_____

_____

_____

_____

What will be my next steps? What can I start, stop, and continue to do?

Additional Resources

Grow Model

The GROW model is a popular coaching framework used to help individuals set and achieve their goals. It was developed in the 1980s by Graham Alexander, Sir John Whitmore, and other experts in the field of coaching.

The acronym GROW stands for:

G	R	O	W
Goal: The first step in the coaching process is to define a specific and measurable goal that the individual wants to achieve. This goal should be challenging, yet realistic and achievable within a set time frame.	Reality: In this step, the individual takes a realistic look at their current situation and identifies any obstacles or challenges that might prevent them from achieving their goal. It's important to be honest and objective during this step in order to develop an effective action plan.	Options: Once the individual has a clear understanding of their current reality, they can begin to identify potential options or strategies for overcoming any obstacles and reaching their goal. This step involves brainstorming and exploring different solutions and approaches.	Way Forward: The final step in the GROW model is to develop a concrete action plan for achieving the goal. This involves identifying specific steps, setting deadlines, and determining how progress will be measured and evaluated.

The GROW model is a simple yet powerful coaching tool that can be used in a variety of contexts, including personal and professional development, career coaching, and team building. By helping individuals focus on specific goals and develop concrete action plans, the GROW model can help them achieve greater success and fulfillment in their lives.

Framework for Problem Solving

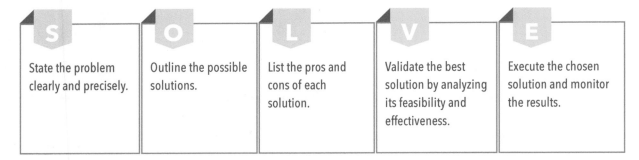

S	**O**	**L**	**V**	**E**
State the problem clearly and precisely.	Outline the possible solutions.	List the pros and cons of each solution.	Validate the best solution by analyzing its feasibility and effectiveness.	Execute the chosen solution and monitor the results.

Framework for Decision Making

1. Identify the problem or decision to be made: Start by clearly defining the problem or decision you need to make. Make sure you have a clear understanding of what needs to be decided and what the goals are.

2. Gather information: Collect all the relevant information you need to make an informed decision. This can include data, research, opinions from experts, and personal experiences.

3. Identify the alternatives: Brainstorm all possible solutions or alternatives to the problem. Evaluate each option based on how well it solves the problem, the risks involved, and the resources required.

4. Evaluate the alternatives: Use the information you gathered to evaluate each alternative. Consider the pros and cons of each option and how well it aligns with your goals.

5. Choose the best alternative: Based on your evaluation, choose the alternative that best solves the problem and aligns with your goals. Make sure you have a clear understanding of the risks and resources required to implement the solution.

6. Implement the decision: Once you have made a decision, create an action plan and implement the solution. Make sure you communicate the decision and action plan to all relevant stakeholders.

7. Evaluate the outcome: After implementing the solution, evaluate the outcome to determine if it was effective in solving the problem. If the solution was not effective, identify what went wrong and learn from it for future decision-making.

DECIDE

D — Define the problem or decision to be made.

E — Explore all possible options and gather information.

C — Consider the pros and cons of each option.

I — Identify the best alternative.

D — Develop an action plan.

E — Execute the plan and implement the decision.

Remember

Decision-making is an iterative process and you may need to revisit and adjust your decisions as new information becomes available.

Feedback Exercise for Self

Start, Stop, and Continue to Do

1. Identify who to ask for feedback: Think about who you would like to ask for feedback. This could be your supervisor, colleagues, clients, or other professionals in your field. You might also consider asking people who work in different departments or areas of your organization.

2. Choose your method of feedback collection: Decide how you want to collect feedback. You could send an email requesting feedback, schedule a one-on-one meeting, or create a survey using an online tool. Consider what method will be most appropriate for the people you're asking and the type of feedback you're looking for.

3. Be specific in your request: In your email or when scheduling a meeting, be clear about what you're asking for. Let the person know that you're looking for feedback on what you can stop doing, start doing, and continue doing to grow professionally. Give them some context for why you're asking for feedback and how you plan to use it.

4. Listen actively: During your meeting or as you read the feedback responses, listen carefully and take notes. Try not to get defensive or dismissive of the feedback, but instead, ask clarifying questions to understand the feedback better. Remember that feedback is an opportunity for growth and development.

5. Organize the feedback: Once you have collected feedback, organize it into categories: stop doing, start doing, and continue doing. Look for common themes or patterns in the feedback to help you identify areas where you can focus your professional growth.

6. Create an action plan: Based on the feedback you have received, create an action plan for what you will stop doing, start doing, and continue doing. Be specific about what steps you will take and when you will take them. Share your action plan with a trusted colleague or mentor and ask for their support and accountability in following through with your plan.

7. **Follow up:** After you have implemented your action plan, follow up with the people who provided feedback and let them know how you have incorporated their suggestions. Ask for their continued support and feedback as you continue to grow professionally.

ACTION PLAN

To achieve your goals, it's essential to have a clear and actionable plan in place. One effective way to do this is by using the A.C.T.I.O.N. acronym.

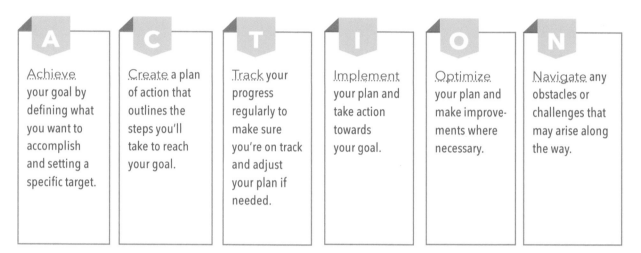

A — Achieve your goal by defining what you want to accomplish and setting a specific target.

C — Create a plan of action that outlines the steps you'll take to reach your goal.

T — Track your progress regularly to make sure you're on track and adjust your plan if needed.

I — Implement your plan and take action towards your goal.

O — Optimize your plan and make improvements where necessary.

N — Navigate any obstacles or challenges that may arise along the way.

The first step is to **Achieve** your goal by defining what you want to accomplish and setting a specific target.

Then, you need to **Create** a plan of action that outlines the steps you'll take to reach your goal.

Next, it's important to **Track** your progress regularly to make sure you're on track and adjust your plan if needed.

Once you have a solid plan in place, it's time to **Implement** it and take action towards your goal.

As you move forward, you should constantly look for ways to **Optimize** your plan and make improvements where necessary.

Finally, be prepared to **Navigate** any obstacles or challenges that may arise along the way. By following the A.C.T.I.O.N. framework, you can stay focused, motivated, and on track towards achieving your goals.

What is your plan of Action moving forward?

....

....

....

....

....

....

....

....

....

....

....

....

....

....

....

Change

The William Bridges Change Model is a framework for managing change in individuals and organizations. The model was developed by William Bridges, a consultant and author who specialized in helping people and organizations navigate transitions.

The model is based on the idea that change is a process that involves three distinct stages: endings, neutral zone, and new beginnings. Here's an overview of each stage:

1. Endings: The first stage of the change process involves letting go of the old ways of doing things. This can be difficult for individuals and organizations because it often means leaving behind familiar routines, relationships, and identities. Endings can be painful and disruptive, but they're also necessary for growth and progress.

2. Neutral Zone: The second stage of the change process is the neutral zone, which is characterized by uncertainty, confusion, and experimentation. In this stage, individuals and organizations are in a state of flux as they try to figure out what the new reality looks like. It can be a challenging time, but it's also an opportunity for creativity and innovation.

3. New Beginnings: The final stage of the change process is new beginnings, where individuals and organizations start to find their footing in the new reality. This stage is marked by a sense of renewed energy and purpose as people begin to implement new ideas and practices.

Throughout the change process, Bridges emphasizes the importance of supporting people and helping them navigate the emotional and psychological challenges of change. This includes acknowledging people's feelings of loss and uncertainty, providing clear communication and guidance, and creating a sense of community and support.

The William Bridges Change Model is widely used in organizations to help manage change and transitions, from mergers and acquisitions to new leadership and strategic initiatives. By understanding the three stages of change and providing support throughout the process, organizations can help ensure successful outcomes and avoid resistance and push back.

1. What are the three stages of the William Bridges Change Model, and how can they help you navigate change?

   ....

   ....

   ....

   ....

2. How can leaders effectively communicate during the "ending" phase of the Bridges Model to help their team process and accept change?

   ....

   ....

   ....

   ....

3. What are some common reactions that individuals experience during the "neutral zone" phase of the Bridges Model, and how can they be managed?

   ....

   ....

   ....

   ....

4. How can you develop a sense of purpose and direction during the "new beginning" phase of the Bridges Model?

   ....

   ....

   ....

   ....

5. What role does resilience play in the Bridges Model, and how can it be developed to help you navigate change?

6. How can you use the Bridges Model to anticipate and prepare for potential challenges during a change initiative?

7. What are some strategies for managing resistance to change during the Bridges Model's "neutral zone" phase?

8. How can you use the Bridges Model to identify and leverage opportunities for growth and development during a change initiative?

9. What are some key considerations for leaders when implementing the Bridges Model to support change within their organization?

....

....

....

....

....

....

10. How can the Bridges Model be adapted to suit the needs of different individuals and teams, and what are some examples of successful adaptations?

....

....

....

....

....

....

....

Resilience

Resilience is the ability to adapt and recover from adversity and challenges. In the workplace, resilience is an essential quality that helps you cope with stress and perform at your best.

Here's a model for resilience in the workplace and some strategies for becoming more resilient:

1. Mindset: Having a positive mindset is the foundation of resilience. It's important to believe that you can overcome challenges and that failure is an opportunity to learn and grow. Adopting a growth mindset can help you develop resilience.

2. Self-Care: Taking care of your physical and emotional well-being is essential for resilience. Make sure you get enough sleep, eat healthy foods, exercise regularly, and take breaks when needed. Practice mindfulness or meditation to help manage stress and anxiety.

3. Social Support: Building and maintaining supportive relationships can help you cope with stress and build resilience. Connect with colleagues, friends, or family members who can provide emotional support and encouragement.

4. Problem-Solving: Being able to identify and solve problems is a critical skill for resilience. Break down problems into smaller parts and identify potential solutions. Be flexible and willing to try new approaches.

5. Adaptability: The ability to adapt to change is essential for resilience. Be open to new ideas and perspectives and be willing to learn new skills. Embrace change as an opportunity for growth.

6. Purpose: Having a sense of purpose and meaning in your work can help you stay motivated and resilient. Connect your work to a larger goal or mission and remind yourself of your values and why your work is important.

Strategies for building resilience:

1. Set realistic goals and prioritize tasks.
2. Practice self-compassion and avoid negative self-talk.
3. Seek feedback and constructive criticism to help you learn and grow.
4. Take breaks and engage in activities that bring you joy.
5. Practice gratitude and focus on the positive aspects of your work.
6. Seek support from colleagues or a professional if needed.

By adopting these strategies and cultivating a resilient mindset, you can overcome challenges and thrive in the workplace.

Powerful Coaching Questions

Asking coaching questions in the workplace can be a powerful tool for developing and supporting employees, promoting self-reflection and growth, and improving overall organizational performance. Here are some reasons why:

Encourages self-reflection: Coaching questions help individuals to think deeply about their experiences, skills, and goals. By asking questions that challenge their assumptions, beliefs, and behaviors, individuals are encouraged to reflect on their strengths and areas for improvement. This can lead to increased self-awareness and a better understanding of their own motivations and aspirations.

Builds trust and rapport: When managers or colleagues ask coaching questions in a non-judgmental and supportive way, it can help to build trust and rapport. By demonstrating a genuine interest in the other person's development and well-being, the questioner creates an environment where individuals feel safe to share their thoughts, concerns, and aspirations.

Promotes learning and development: Coaching questions can be used to encourage individuals to explore new ideas, approaches, and perspectives. By challenging individuals to think creatively and critically, coaching questions can help to foster a culture of continuous learning and development within the workplace.

Encourages problem-solving: Coaching questions can help individuals to identify and address problems, obstacles, and challenges in a proactive and constructive way. By focusing on solutions rather than blame, coaching questions can help to promote a growth mindset and a sense of ownership over one's own development and performance.

Improves communication skills: Coaching questions can help individuals to develop their communication skills by encouraging active listening, empathetic responding, and effective questioning. By practicing these skills, individuals can become better communicators and collaborators, which can have a positive impact on teamwork and overall organizational performance.

Asking coaching questions in the workplace can be a powerful tool for promoting self-reflection, building trust and rapport, promoting learning and development, encouraging problem-solving, and improving communication skills. By incorporating coaching questions into their leadership style, managers and colleagues can create a supportive and empowering environment that fosters growth and development for all.

Sample Coaching Questions

1. What is your biggest challenge right now?
2. What are your goals for this project?
3. What resources do you need to achieve your goals?
4. How can I support you in achieving your goals?
5. What obstacles are you facing, and how can you overcome them?
6. What are your strengths and how can you leverage them to achieve your goals?
7. What are your areas for improvement, and how can you work on them?
8. What would success look like for you in this situation?
9. How can you approach this situation differently to achieve a better outcome?
10. What is the next step you need to take to move forward?
11. What have you learned from this experience, and how can you apply it in the future?
12. What are the potential risks involved in this decision, and how can you mitigate them?
13. How can you communicate more effectively with your team members?
14. What can you do to improve your time management and prioritize your tasks?
15. How can you maintain a positive attitude and stay motivated in the face of challenges?

"I'VE LEARNED THAT PEOPLE WILL FORGET WHAT YOU SAID, PEOPLE WILL FORGET WHAT YOU DID, BUT PEOPLE WILL NEVER FORGET HOW YOU MADE THEM FEEL."

—MAYA ANGELOU.

Coaching Session
Notes

Date

Session#

Session Topics

Updates and Progress
from Last Session

_____
_____
_____
_____
_____
_____
_____

Session Notes

Homework

Action Items

_____
_____
_____
_____
_____

_____
_____
_____
_____
_____

Date

Session#

Session Topics

Updates and Progress from Last Session

Session Notes

Homework

Action Items

Date

Session Topics

Updates and Progress from Last Session

Session Notes

Homework

Action Items

Date

Session#

Session Topics

....
....
....
....
....
....

Updates and Progress from Last Session

Session Notes

Homework

....
....
....
....
....

Action Items

....
....
....
....
....

Date

Session#

Session Topics

....
....
....
....
....
....
....

Updates and Progress
from Last Session

Session Notes

Homework

....
....
....
....

Action Items

....
....
....
....

Date

Session#

Session Topics

Updates and Progress
from Last Session

Session Notes

Homework

Action Items

Date

Session#

Session Topics

....
....
....
....
....
....

Updates and Progress
from Last Session

Session Notes

Homework

....
....
....
....

Action Items

....
....
....
....

Date

Session #

Session Topics

Updates and Progress from Last Session

Session Notes

Homework

Action Items

Date

Session#

Session Topics

Updates and Progress
from Last Session

....
....
....
....
....
....
....

Session Notes

Homework

....
....
....
....
....

Action Items

....
....
....
....
....

Date

Session#

Session Topics

....
....
....
....
....
....

Updates and Progress from Last Session

Session Notes

Homework

....
....
....
....

Action Items

....
....
....
....

Date

Session#

Session Topics

....
....
....
....
....
....
....

Updates and Progress from Last Session

Session Notes

Homework

....
....
....
....
....

Action Items

....
....
....
....
....

Date

Session#

Session Topics

....

....

....

....

....

....

Updates and Progress from Last Session

Session Notes

Homework

....

....

....

....

....

Action Items

....

....

....

....

....

Date

Session#

Session Topics

Updates and Progress from Last Session

....

....

....

....

....

....

Session Notes

Homework

....

....

....

....

Action Items

....

....

....

....

Date

Session#

Session Topics

....
....
....
....
....
....
....

Updates and Progress from Last Session

Session Notes

Homework

....
....
....
....
....

Action Items

....
....
....
....
....

Date

Session#

Session Topics

Updates and Progress
from Last Session

....

....

....

....

....

....

Session Notes

Homework

....

....

....

....

Action Items

....

....

....

....

Date

Session#

Session Topics

Updates and Progress from Last Session

Session Notes

Homework

Action Items

Date

Session Topics

....
....
....
....
....
....

Updates and Progress
from Last Session

Session Notes

Homework

....
....
....
....

Action Items

....
....
....
....

Date

Session#

Session Topics

Updates and Progress from Last Session

Session Notes

Homework

Action Items

Date

Session#

Session Topics

....
....
....
....
....
....

Updates and Progress from Last Session

Session Notes

Homework

....
....
....
....

Action Items

....
....
....
....

Date

Session#

Session Topics

Updates and Progress
from Last Session

Session Notes

Homework

Action Items

"TELL ME, WHAT
IS IT YOU PLAN TO
DO WITH YOUR
ONE WILD AND
PRECIOUS LIFE?"

–MARY OLIVER

Weekly
Reflections

What progress have you made since our last coaching session, and what obstacles have you encountered?

....

....

....

What insights or new perspectives did you gain from our last coaching session, and how have you applied them to your work or life?

....

....

....

What goals did you set for yourself after our last coaching session, and how are you progressing toward them?

....

....

....

What new challenges or opportunities have emerged since our last coaching session, and how are you approaching them?

....

....

....

How have you been practicing the skills or behaviors we discussed in our last coaching session, and what results have you seen?

....

....

....

What feedback have you received from others since our last coaching session, and how have you incorporated that feedback into your growth plan?

....

....

....

What questions or concerns do you have about your progress or development, and how can we address them in our next coaching session?

....

....

....

Date: ....   Session#: ....

What progress have you made since our last coaching session, and what obstacles have you encountered?

....

....

....

What insights or new perspectives did you gain from our last coaching session, and how have you applied them to your work or life?

....

....

....

What goals did you set for yourself after our last coaching session, and how are you progressing toward them?

....

....

....

What new challenges or opportunities have emerged since our last coaching session, and how are you approaching them?

....

....

....

How have you been practicing the skills or behaviors we discussed in our last coaching session, and what results have you seen?

....

....

....

What feedback have you received from others since our last coaching session, and how have you incorporated that feedback into your growth plan?

....

....

....

What questions or concerns do you have about your progress or development, and how can we address them in our next coaching session?

....

....

....

What progress have you made since our last coaching session, and what obstacles have you encountered?

....
....
....

What insights or new perspectives did you gain from our last coaching session, and how have you applied them to your work or life?

....
....
....

What goals did you set for yourself after our last coaching session, and how are you progressing toward them?

....
....
....

What new challenges or opportunities have emerged since our last coaching session, and how are you approaching them?

....
....
....

How have you been practicing the skills or behaviors we discussed in our last coaching session, and what results have you seen?

....
....
....

What feedback have you received from others since our last coaching session, and how have you incorporated that feedback into your growth plan?

....
....
....

What questions or concerns do you have about your progress or development, and how can we address them in our next coaching session?

....
....
....

Date: ....   Session#: ....

What progress have you made since our last coaching session, and what obstacles have you encountered?

....
....
....

What insights or new perspectives did you gain from our last coaching session, and how have you applied them to your work or life?

....
....
....

What goals did you set for yourself after our last coaching session, and how are you progressing toward them?

....
....
....

What new challenges or opportunities have emerged since our last coaching session, and how are you approaching them?

....
....
....

How have you been practicing the skills or behaviors we discussed in our last coaching session, and what results have you seen?

....
....
....

What feedback have you received from others since our last coaching session, and how have you incorporated that feedback into your growth plan?

....
....
....

What questions or concerns do you have about your progress or development, and how can we address them in our next coaching session?

....
....

What progress have you made since our last coaching session, and what obstacles have you encountered?

....

....

....

What insights or new perspectives did you gain from our last coaching session, and how have you applied them to your work or life?

....

....

....

What goals did you set for yourself after our last coaching session, and how are you progressing toward them?

....

....

....

What new challenges or opportunities have emerged since our last coaching session, and how are you approaching them?

....

....

....

How have you been practicing the skills or behaviors we discussed in our last coaching session, and what results have you seen?

....

....

....

What feedback have you received from others since our last coaching session, and how have you incorporated that feedback into your growth plan?

....

....

....

What questions or concerns do you have about your progress or development, and how can we address them in our next coaching session?

....

....

....

Date: .... Session#: ....

What progress have you made since our last coaching session, and what obstacles have you encountered?

....

....

....

What insights or new perspectives did you gain from our last coaching session, and how have you applied them to your work or life?

....

....

....

What goals did you set for yourself after our last coaching session, and how are you progressing toward them?

....

....

....

What new challenges or opportunities have emerged since our last coaching session, and how are you approaching them?

....

....

....

How have you been practicing the skills or behaviors we discussed in our last coaching session, and what results have you seen?

....

....

....

What feedback have you received from others since our last coaching session, and how have you incorporated that feedback into your growth plan?

....

....

....

What questions or concerns do you have about your progress or development, and how can we address them in our next coaching session?

....

....

....

What progress have you made since our last coaching session, and what obstacles have you encountered?

....
....
....

What insights or new perspectives did you gain from our last coaching session, and how have you applied them to your work or life?

....
....
....

What goals did you set for yourself after our last coaching session, and how are you progressing toward them?

....
....
....

What new challenges or opportunities have emerged since our last coaching session, and how are you approaching them?

....
....
....

How have you been practicing the skills or behaviors we discussed in our last coaching session, and what results have you seen?

....
....
....

What feedback have you received from others since our last coaching session, and how have you incorporated that feedback into your growth plan?

....
....
....

What questions or concerns do you have about your progress or development, and how can we address them in our next coaching session?

....
....
....

Date: .... Session#: ....

What progress have you made since our last coaching session, and what obstacles have you encountered?

....

....

....

What insights or new perspectives did you gain from our last coaching session, and how have you applied them to your work or life?

....

....

....

What goals did you set for yourself after our last coaching session, and how are you progressing toward them?

....

....

....

What new challenges or opportunities have emerged since our last coaching session, and how are you approaching them?

....

....

....

How have you been practicing the skills or behaviors we discussed in our last coaching session, and what results have you seen?

....

....

....

What feedback have you received from others since our last coaching session, and how have you incorporated that feedback into your growth plan?

....

....

....

What questions or concerns do you have about your progress or development, and how can we address them in our next coaching session?

....

....

....

What progress have you made since our last coaching session, and what obstacles have you encountered?

....
....
....

What insights or new perspectives did you gain from our last coaching session, and how have you applied them to your work or life?

....
....
....

What goals did you set for yourself after our last coaching session, and how are you progressing toward them?

....
....
....

What new challenges or opportunities have emerged since our last coaching session, and how are you approaching them?

....
....
....

How have you been practicing the skills or behaviors we discussed in our last coaching session, and what results have you seen?

....
....
....

What feedback have you received from others since our last coaching session, and how have you incorporated that feedback into your growth plan?

....
....
....

What questions or concerns do you have about your progress or development, and how can we address them in our next coaching session?

....
....
....

Date: .... Session#: ....

What progress have you made since our last coaching session, and what obstacles have you encountered?

....

....

....

What insights or new perspectives did you gain from our last coaching session, and how have you applied them to your work or life?

....

....

....

What goals did you set for yourself after our last coaching session, and how are you progressing toward them?

....

....

....

What new challenges or opportunities have emerged since our last coaching session, and how are you approaching them?

....

....

....

How have you been practicing the skills or behaviors we discussed in our last coaching session, and what results have you seen?

....

....

....

What feedback have you received from others since our last coaching session, and how have you incorporated that feedback into your growth plan?

....

....

....

What questions or concerns do you have about your progress or development, and how can we address them in our next coaching session?

....

....

....

Date: .... Session#: ....

What progress have you made since our last coaching session, and what obstacles have you encountered?

....

....

....

What insights or new perspectives did you gain from our last coaching session, and how have you applied them to your work or life?

....

....

....

What goals did you set for yourself after our last coaching session, and how are you progressing toward them?

....

....

....

What new challenges or opportunities have emerged since our last coaching session, and how are you approaching them?

....

....

....

How have you been practicing the skills or behaviors we discussed in our last coaching session, and what results have you seen?

....

....

....

What feedback have you received from others since our last coaching session, and how have you incorporated that feedback into your growth plan?

....

....

....

What questions or concerns do you have about your progress or development, and how can we address them in our next coaching session?

....

....

....

Date: .... Session#: ....

What progress have you made since our last coaching session, and what obstacles have you encountered?

....

....

....

What insights or new perspectives did you gain from our last coaching session, and how have you applied them to your work or life?

....

....

....

What goals did you set for yourself after our last coaching session, and how are you progressing toward them?

....

....

....

What new challenges or opportunities have emerged since our last coaching session, and how are you approaching them?

....

....

....

How have you been practicing the skills or behaviors we discussed in our last coaching session, and what results have you seen?

....

....

....

What feedback have you received from others since our last coaching session, and how have you incorporated that feedback into your growth plan?

....

....

....

What questions or concerns do you have about your progress or development, and how can we address them in our next coaching session?

....

....

....

What progress have you made since our last coaching session, and what obstacles have you encountered?

....

....

....

What insights or new perspectives did you gain from our last coaching session, and how have you applied them to your work or life?

....

....

....

What goals did you set for yourself after our last coaching session, and how are you progressing toward them?

....

....

....

What new challenges or opportunities have emerged since our last coaching session, and how are you approaching them?

....

....

....

How have you been practicing the skills or behaviors we discussed in our last coaching session, and what results have you seen?

....

....

....

What feedback have you received from others since our last coaching session, and how have you incorporated that feedback into your growth plan?

....

....

....

What questions or concerns do you have about your progress or development, and how can we address them in our next coaching session?

....

....

....

Date: .... Session#: ....

What progress have you made since our last coaching session, and what obstacles have you encountered?

....
....
....

What insights or new perspectives did you gain from our last coaching session, and how have you applied them to your work or life?

....
....
....

What goals did you set for yourself after our last coaching session, and how are you progressing toward them?

....
....
....

What new challenges or opportunities have emerged since our last coaching session, and how are you approaching them?

....
....
....

How have you been practicing the skills or behaviors we discussed in our last coaching session, and what results have you seen?

....
....
....

What feedback have you received from others since our last coaching session, and how have you incorporated that feedback into your growth plan?

....
....
....

What questions or concerns do you have about your progress or development, and how can we address them in our next coaching session?

....
....
....

What progress have you made since our last coaching session, and what obstacles have you encountered?

....

....

....

What insights or new perspectives did you gain from our last coaching session, and how have you applied them to your work or life?

....

....

....

What goals did you set for yourself after our last coaching session, and how are you progressing toward them?

....

....

....

What new challenges or opportunities have emerged since our last coaching session, and how are you approaching them?

....

....

....

How have you been practicing the skills or behaviors we discussed in our last coaching session, and what results have you seen?

....

....

....

What feedback have you received from others since our last coaching session, and how have you incorporated that feedback into your growth plan?

....

....

....

What questions or concerns do you have about your progress or development, and how can we address them in our next coaching session?

....

....

....

Date: .... Session#: ....

What progress have you made since our last coaching session, and what obstacles have you encountered?

....

....

....

What insights or new perspectives did you gain from our last coaching session, and how have you applied them to your work or life?

....

....

....

What goals did you set for yourself after our last coaching session, and how are you progressing toward them?

....

....

....

What new challenges or opportunities have emerged since our last coaching session, and how are you approaching them?

....

....

....

How have you been practicing the skills or behaviors we discussed in our last coaching session, and what results have you seen?

....

....

....

What feedback have you received from others since our last coaching session, and how have you incorporated that feedback into your growth plan?

....

....

....

What questions or concerns do you have about your progress or development, and how can we address them in our next coaching session?

....

....

....

What progress have you made since our last coaching session, and what obstacles have you encountered?

....
....
....

What insights or new perspectives did you gain from our last coaching session, and how have you applied them to your work or life?

....
....
....

What goals did you set for yourself after our last coaching session, and how are you progressing toward them?

....
....
....

What new challenges or opportunities have emerged since our last coaching session, and how are you approaching them?

....
....
....

How have you been practicing the skills or behaviors we discussed in our last coaching session, and what results have you seen?

....
....
....

What feedback have you received from others since our last coaching session, and how have you incorporated that feedback into your growth plan?

....
....
....

What questions or concerns do you have about your progress or development, and how can we address them in our next coaching session?

....
....
....

Date: .... Session#: ....

What progress have you made since our last coaching session, and what obstacles have you encountered?

....

....

....

What insights or new perspectives did you gain from our last coaching session, and how have you applied them to your work or life?

....

....

....

What goals did you set for yourself after our last coaching session, and how are you progressing toward them?

....

....

....

What new challenges or opportunities have emerged since our last coaching session, and how are you approaching them?

....

....

....

How have you been practicing the skills or behaviors we discussed in our last coaching session, and what results have you seen?

....

....

....

What feedback have you received from others since our last coaching session, and how have you incorporated that feedback into your growth plan?

....

....

....

What questions or concerns do you have about your progress or development, and how can we address them in our next coaching session?

....

....

....

What progress have you made since our last coaching session, and what obstacles have you encountered?

....

....

....

What insights or new perspectives did you gain from our last coaching session, and how have you applied them to your work or life?

....

....

....

What goals did you set for yourself after our last coaching session, and how are you progressing toward them?

....

....

....

What new challenges or opportunities have emerged since our last coaching session, and how are you approaching them?

....

....

....

How have you been practicing the skills or behaviors we discussed in our last coaching session, and what results have you seen?

....

....

....

What feedback have you received from others since our last coaching session, and how have you incorporated that feedback into your growth plan?

....

....

....

What questions or concerns do you have about your progress or development, and how can we address them in our next coaching session?

....

....

....

Date: .... Session#: ....

What progress have you made since our last coaching session, and what obstacles have you encountered?

....

....

....

What insights or new perspectives did you gain from our last coaching session, and how have you applied them to your work or life?

....

....

....

What goals did you set for yourself after our last coaching session, and how are you progressing toward them?

....

....

....

What new challenges or opportunities have emerged since our last coaching session, and how are you approaching them?

....

....

....

How have you been practicing the skills or behaviors we discussed in our last coaching session, and what results have you seen?

....

....

....

What feedback have you received from others since our last coaching session, and how have you incorporated that feedback into your growth plan?

....

....

....

What questions or concerns do you have about your progress or development, and how can we address them in our next coaching session?

....

....

What progress have you made since our last coaching session, and what obstacles have you encountered?

....
....
....

What insights or new perspectives did you gain from our last coaching session, and how have you applied them to your work or life?

....
....
....

What goals did you set for yourself after our last coaching session, and how are you progressing toward them?

....
....
....

What new challenges or opportunities have emerged since our last coaching session, and how are you approaching them?

....
....
....

How have you been practicing the skills or behaviors we discussed in our last coaching session, and what results have you seen?

....
....
....

What feedback have you received from others since our last coaching session, and how have you incorporated that feedback into your growth plan?

....
....
....

What questions or concerns do you have about your progress or development, and how can we address them in our next coaching session?

....
....
....

Printed in the USA
CPSIA information can be obtained
at www.ICGtesting.com
LVHW061132261023
762209LV00044B/716